The Wine Lover Cooks **Italian**

D1318481

The Wine Lover Cooks **Italian**

Pairing Great Recipes with
the Perfect Glass of Wine

by Brian St. Pierre

Photographs by Minh + Wass

CHRONICLE BOOKS

SAN FRANCISCO

LIBRARY OF CONGRESS CATALOGING-IN-PUBLICATION-DATA:

ST. PIERRE, BRIAN.

THE WINE LOVER COOKS ITALIAN : PAIRING GREAT RECIPES WITH THE PERFECT

GLASS OF WINE / BY BRIAN ST. PIERRE ; PHOTOGRAPHS BY MINH + WASS.

   P. CM.

INCLUDES INDEX.

ISBN 0-8118-4100-6 (PBK.)

1. COOKERY, ITALIAN. 2. COOKERY (WINE) I. TITLE: PAIRING GREAT RECIPES WITH

THE PERFECT GLASS OF WINE. II. TITLE.

TX723.S695 2005

641.5945—DC22

   2004023249

MANUFACTURED IN SINGAPORE.

DESIGNED BY RICK RAWLINS/WORK

PROP STYLING BY NGOC MINH NGO

FOOD STYLING BY SUSIE THEODOROU

THE PHOTOGRAPHER WISHES TO THANK

ANNIE & TRONG FOR THEIR HOSPITALITY

DISTRIBUTED IN CANADA BY RAINCOAST BOOKS

   9050 SHAUGHNESSY STREET

   VANCOUVER, BRITISH COLUMBIA V6P 6E5

10 9 8 7 6 5 4 3 2 1

CHRONICLE BOOKS LLC

   85 SECOND STREET

   SAN FRANCISCO, CALIFORNIA 94105

   WWW.CHRONICLEBOOKS.COM

For my son Patrick, better late than never,

never too late.

Acknowledgments

Falling in love with Italy is a quick and easy process; working there is a lot more complicated. Luckily, I had friends, and acquired more, who were generous with their time, thoughts, recipes, cooking tips and techniques, wine and wine knowledge, and, above all, their stories. Over several years, as this book built up, layer by layer, I had special reason to thank the following people.

Wineries (Italy): Piero Antinori, Marchese L&P Antinori, Florence; Roberto and Paolo Bava, Cantine Bava, Cocconato, Piedmont; Pio Boffa, Pio Cesare Winery, Alba, Piedmont; Sandro Boscaini and Tiziana Ravanelli, Masi Agricola, Verona; Pier Francesco Bolla, Agricola Boltina, Montiano; Riccardo Cotarella, Azienda Vinicola Falesco, Montefiascone, Lazio; Adolfo Folonari, Ruffino, Brescia; Diana Frescobaldi, Marchesi de'Frescobaldi, Florence; Angelo Gaja, Barbaresco, Piedmont; Marta Gaspari, Donnafugata, Marsala, Sicily; Chiara Gianotti, Fazi Battaglia, Castelpiano, Marche; Lars Leicht, Villa Banfi, Montalcino, Tuscany; Teresa Severini Lungarotti, Cantine Lungarotti, Torgiano, Umbria; Fausto Maculan, Breganze, Veneto; Mark Shannon and Elvezia Sbalchiero, A Mano Winery, Castellaneta, Puglia; Aldo, Milena, and Giuseppe Vaira, GD Vajra Winery, Barolo, Piedmont; Antonio M. Zaccheo Sr. and Jr., Carpineto, Greve in Chianti, Tuscany.

Wineries (California): Francis Ford Coppola, Niebaum-Coppola, Rutherford; Joel Ehrlich, chef at Viansa in Sonoma, and Sam and Vicky Sebastiani, Viansa Winery, Carneros; Ed Seghesio and the Seghesio family, Seghesio Winery, Healdsburg.

Chefs and restauranteurs: Bruno Barbieri, Ristorante Arquade, Hotel Villa del Quar, Verona; Luca di Vita and Bruno Gavagnin, Alle Testiere, Venice; Fulvio Ferri, Vetralla, Lazio; Susanna Gelmetti, London and various Italian locations by *Italian Cookery Weeks*; Alvaro Maccioni, La Famiglia restaurant, London, and Coselli School of Tuscan Cuisine, Coselli, Tuscany; Eilidh MacDonald and Giancarlo Talerico, Rhode School of Cuisine at Villa Lucia, Vorno, Tuscany; Gabriele Monti, Ristorante Vecchia Urbino, Urbino; Valentina Morriconi and chef Antonio Martucci, International Wine Academy of Rome; Lucio Sforza, L'Asino d'Oro, Orvieto; Franco and Melly Solari, Cà Peo, Leivi, Genoa, Liguria; Luciano Sona and Mauro Chieregati, Les Clochards, Verona; Arnold Eric Wong and Debbie Zachareas, Bacar Restaurant, San Francisco, California.

Hosts: Roberta Berni, Azienda di Promozione Turistica, Florence; Rita Compagnoni, Sestre Levante, Liguria; Federica Crocetta and Antonio Rosati, Le Querce, Carpegna, Marche; Rosanna Faggiani and Corrado de Luca, Marta, Lake Bolsena, Lazio; Janina Mathiasz, Veronafiere/ Vinitaly, Verona; Alison and Stephen Rudgard, Rome.

Sources: Richard Baudains and Giles Watson, Friuli; Alessandra Bottaro, Italian Trade Commission, London; Consorzio Tutela Vini Valdadige, Verona; Consorzio Tutela Montasio, Udine, Friuli; Consorzio Formaggio Monte Veronese, Verona; Consorzio Tutela Extravergine d'Oliva Garda, Bardolino, Verona; Consorzio Tutela Vini Valpolicella, San Floriano, Verona; Mary Jane Cryan, Vetralla, Lazio; Paola Frabetti, Unione Camere Regione Emilia-Romagna, Bologna; David Gleave MW, Liberty Wines, London; Matt Kramer in Venice; Cliff Nicholson, London; Dacotah Renneau, London; Ursula Thurner, Florence.

Special thanks for knowledge, help, contacts, and optimism to Francesca Blench, Grand Heritage International, Varallo, Tuscany; esteemed colleague Michele Shah, Arezzo, Tuscany; and Stephen Hobley, *Decanter* magazine's ambassador-at-large to Italy. Back in the mists of time, Doreen Schmid and Darrell Corti helped propel me in this direction, and I can never thank them enough.

B. St.P.

Contents : Introduction

: Italian Wine and Food

: Foundations

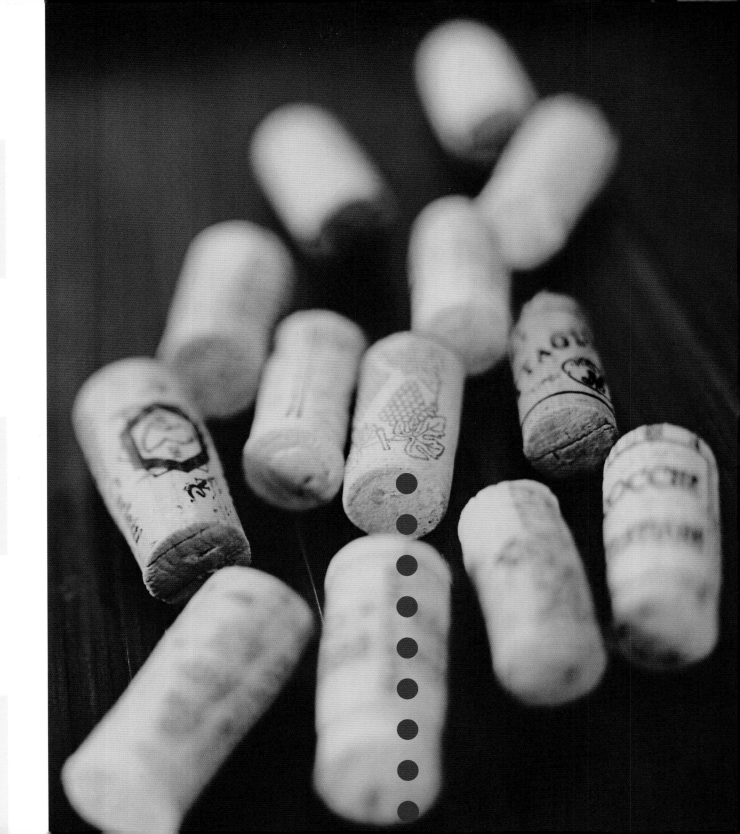

Introduction

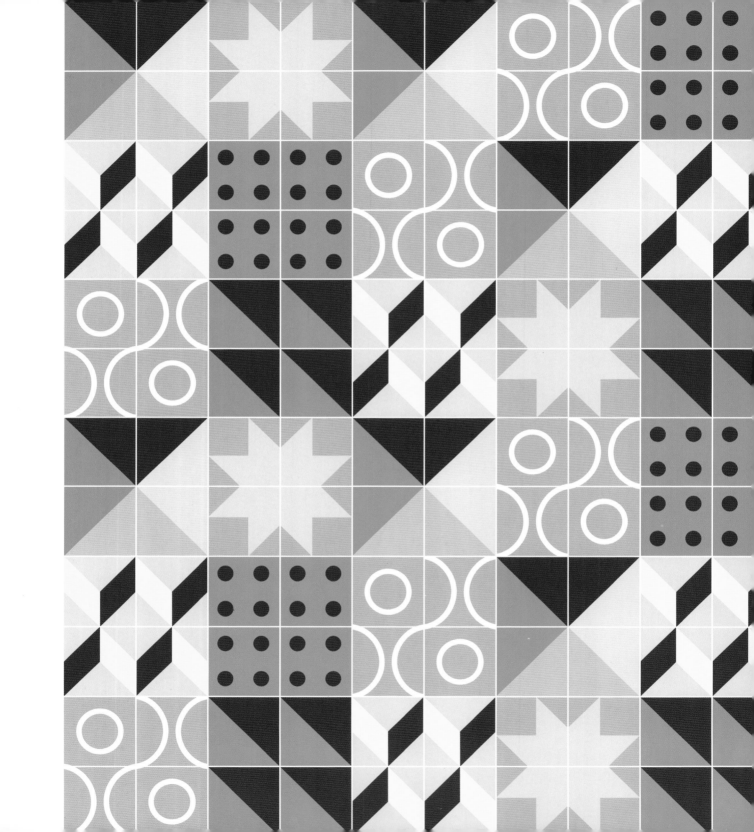

Italian Wine : The New Renaissance

More than five hundred years ago, Italy lifted itself and Europe out of the long, gloomy funk of the Middle Ages with the brightly illuminating sunshine of the Renaissance, a long-lasting, generous gift that went far beyond notions of art and beauty. It may have been dented and smudged from time to time, but the ideal of perspective, of harmony and balance is still with us. Italy has been knocked around since then, too, but it's still standing, and still exporting good ideas. The newest one, which may seem odd because the Italians have been at it for more than four thousand years, is wine. But this is modern Italian wine, another renaissance in the making, a considerable sensual and intellectual liberation from another kind of gloomy funk, a dull global swamp of increasingly standardized wine, a potentially joyless, conformist trend threatening to pull down a lot of other ideals, gastronomic and otherwise. The Italian winemakers who are exuberantly going their own way have provided us another generous gift, ours for the taking here and now, no strings attached, right on the end of our corkscrews.

When the ancient Greeks conquered southern Italy, they called it Enotria, the "land of wine," for the grapevines that grew there in wild profusion. The Greeks organized things a bit better, and taught the locals how to cultivate vineyards, and then the Romans elevated winemaking to something of an art. Roman armies took vine cuttings and seeds with them as they conquered much of the rest of Europe, planting vineyards wherever they went (wine was often safer than the local water, but they also believed in its medicinal properties).

When the barbarians invaded Italy and crushed much of it into the Dark Ages, the outposts of the former empire, especially France and Germany, pressed on.

Eventually, the cycle came around again and Italy's wines flourished alongside the rise of spectacular gastronomy, lubricated the Renaissance, and even created fortunes, as ships were built to carry wine to Belgium, Germany, and England (the British paid luxury prices for what was then known as Florence red, a precursor to Chianti, and Vernaccia, then slightly sweet and high in alcohol). Italy's European neighbors carried out the subsequent round of invasions over the next couple of hundred years, actions not always so devastating to the local culture.

One of the things that climbed through the window of opportunity between wars in the eighteenth and nineteenth centuries was the produce of the New World: tomatoes, potatoes, turkeys, chocolate, peppers, vanilla, sugar, and corn. Europeans took some of them into the kitchen, usually cautiously; Italians took them all and, with the ingenuity they still display, transformed them into Italian cuisine.

In 1861, Italy became a unified nation rather than a jigsaw puzzle of republics, dukedoms, principalities, city-states, and protectorates. For a brief time, Florence was the capital of Italy, and the creator of the formula for blending Chianti, Baron Ricasoli, was prime minister. With stability and prosperity, wine dynasties began on other great estates. Within a decade, Italy's wine production doubled, corks began to be used widely in bottles, and the modern era began.

The estate system continued for nearly a hundred years. In the end, it was flawed, creating not only problems it took another generation to solve, but also a confused image for Italian wine. The system had been based on sharecroppers working the farms and living on a percentage of the crops they raised—an incentive to quantity, not quality, on many estates where the landowners were more interested in cash than pride. The surpluses, and inconsistent wine, continued until the 1960s, when the estates were broken up. The next generation took over in a more businesslike way, and Italy's first set of national wine laws was written, establishing controlled denominations of origin (DOC) and the beginning of standards for vineyards and winemaking.

Change was erratic and slow, the laws were rewritten several times, and expanding exports brought in the rest of the world, sometimes with uncomfortable nontraditional ideas. There were generational shifts, with the winemakers' children going off to work for a season in wineries in the Napa Valley or Bordeaux and returning bursting with ideas for expensive modernization, new wine blends, and promotional gimmicks. Bureaucrats from the European Union changed the rules, not always for the better. Through it all, sometimes because of this push and pull, sometimes despite it, Italian wine was steadily evolving. Italy had the soil and sunshine and great grapes, and now money, sophistication, and technology began to complete the equation. In 1988, Italian wine production finally began to decrease, as the Italians, and the rest of us, began drinking less, but better. The trend has continued.

Matching
Italian Wine and Food

When it comes to Italian wine and food, the "rules" are the same as with any other cuisine: what gives pleasure? In a way, the whole idea is even easier, as the wine and food have grown up together for centuries. Obviously, the best way to decide about good matches is simply to taste, and decide what you like (but try everything). There are some differences between some Italian wines and the other wines of the world, however, which is less of a problem than an opportunity.

White wines aren't as highly regarded in Italy as they are elsewhere around the globe. Most of the ones from Italian grapes are fairly subtle, not blockbusters. Most of them go well enough with food, just not with big, richly flavored food, and they are at least always pleasant, sometimes a lot more. New technology, especially cold fermentation in stainless-steel tanks, has enabled more flavor to be teased out of them, and when the wines are blended, rather than from a single grape, the blends are getting more sophisticated. Indeed, very often these modern Italian whites are more flavorful because of the virtues several grapes bring to the party: one for aroma, another for crisp acidity, a third for body.

There are, increasingly, wines made from grapes that originated in France, especially Chardonnay, a relative new-comer among the whites. A global economy creates all sorts of standardized products, including wine, and Italy unfortunately has no shortage of Chardonnays that are so swathed in oak that they taste of wood and butterscotch and tropical fruit, just like the Chardonnays of California and Australia. This is what is known as the international style, made in many countries. If they're what you fancy, you'll fancy them. On the other hand, there are some interesting, more subtle Chardonnay blends with native Italian grapes, especially from Sicily, that have some Italian character and are worth trying. The popular Pinot Grigio and Sauvignon Blanc are a different story. Introduced in Italy in the nineteenth century, they seem to have gone native, at least acquiring a benign Italian character all their own.

Reds are often glorious, with supple, sinewy verve and bite, often full bodied and elegant, but Italy is also becoming the last refuge of something the world badly needs: light, refreshing red wine that tastes of the grape that made it and the land it comes from, rather than of the oak barrel in which it was aged—wine that doesn't tire out your palate or make your gums ache. Once again, there is no shortage of bold Cabernet Sauvignons and musclebound Merlots in the international blockbuster style, but few other countries have the same sort of range of unique, fascinating red wines, from light and cheery Valpolicella up through savory middleweights like Dolcetto, Negroamaro, Nero d'Avola, and Barbera, to the seriousness of Chianti, Barolo, and Aglianico, and that's only half the story. There are other grapes, and an abundance of blends, in delicious profusion.

Red or white, those international-style wines don't pair as well with Italian or even Italian-style food as Italian wines do. They're too overbearing, not accommodating enough to be good partners. Taking charge is one thing for a police officer or a general, but it's another for a wine.

The French have a useful term for the individualism of specific places: they speak, especially with regard to agriculture, of *terroir*. Literally, it means "soil," with a secondary definition of "homeland," but when it comes to wine and food, it's defined as the ecology of a place—the soil, the rainfall and sunshine, temperature patterns, which way the wind blows, and anything else that contributes to the environmental bundle, especially anything that shapes the nature of the crop. Grapes grow in temperate zones all over the world because they're adaptable, and when they get themselves sorted out in a particular *terroir* (there really is no right word in Italian or English), they reflect that place in their flavors. Sangiovese from Tuscany, the basis of Chianti, tastes different from Sangiovese from Liguria, Emilia-Romagna, Umbria, or any of the other places it thrives. Pinot Grigio has as many nuances as the hillsides it grows on. The wines also fit in with the cuisine of the place, as they're sharing the *terroir* with the fruits and vegetables that are cultivated there. They've grown up together, after all. The neighborhood is the context.

By now, nearly everybody knows that Italian food isn't all tomato sauce and garlic and pasta, that it can be subtle, stylish, inventive, and complex. Regionality still rules, and there's a strong sense of tradition, so that as the local cuisines have evolved, the local wines have too, in step, as partners. In this book, I've selected food to match the wines on that basis, with ideas and recipes either from local chefs, cooking teachers, winemakers, or home cooks I've talked with, or, in a few cases, modern adaptations of classic regional dishes. The aim was always harmony and balance of food and wine. In some instances, I've indicated good matches with either white or red wines for the same foods. I couldn't have done that with the wines of most other countries, which simply aren't as versatile. The best Italian cuisine has a bit of modesty, even when it's showing off. The land of the beautiful gesture, *la bella figura,* has a sense of proportion.

About This Book

The recipes in this book are organized geographically, in six sections (plus dessert), from west to east across northern Italy, then the center of the country, the eastern coast along the Adriatic Sea, the south, and the islands offshore. Each section has a brief explanation of the character and the gastronomy of the regions within it, followed by notes on the principal wines of the regions. The wines are listed in order of prominence, with the most important first. Most of them have a note on the typical aromas and flavors that may be found in that wine, intended as a rough guide to its style and character, and then some tips on matching the wine with food, Italian and sometimes otherwise. Some of them, especially a few of the light whites, are simply sketched in. They exist to be enjoyed on simple, easy terms—casual social occasions and lunches—and any extended analysis would be close to preposterous.

Not every Italian wine or wine type is included here. There are hundreds of grape varieties grown in Italy, used to make thousands of different wines. Most don't travel very far. I've described the ones that do, including a few rising stars. I've also mostly concentrated on the Italian varieties, or wines like Pinot Grigio that have acquired Italian character and style over the course of more than a hundred years of acclimatization. International varieties, such as Chardonnay or Merlot, don't show enough different character to be very interesting.

Dessert wines transcend regionality. These luscious sweeties are the one class of wine that isn't necessarily bound by borders. Every region of Italy has a version of the local wine that is set aside to be made into something sweet, and a few of these have become famous enough to travel widely. I've selected a few dessert recipes that show them off, and grouped them together after the geographical sections.

At the end of the book is a short section of basic recipes that are staple ingredients, or so-called building blocks, in many of my recipes. You are certain to find uses for them beyond this book. Finally, olive oil matters to Italian wine, too, so there are notes on it, along with a brief survey of Italian cheese, which can be glorious. The index is the best place to look for specific foods, and for wines, organized alphabetically rather than geographically.

Glossary of Italian Wine Terms

Italian wine labels can be confusing, as many of them mix dialect words with generally unfamiliar terms, or add colorful touches with fanciful language. Here are some key words to help you find your way through the information thicket.

Abboccato
Just lightly sweet, but rounded, mouth filling.

Alberello
Bush; used to describe a method of training grapevines in a low, free-standing manner, common in southern Italy.

Amabile
Medium sweet.

Amaro
Bitter; used to describe the aftertaste of some wines, and not necessarily negative when applied to some dry red wines.

Annata
Vintage year.

Appassimento
The method of drying grapes, usually in lofts on straw or plastic mats, to concentrate their sugars and flavor; usually used for sweet wines.

Azienda agricola
A winery or estate that makes wine that uses a minimum of 50 percent of its own cultivated grapes (the remainder may be purchased or brought in from other properties).

Barrique
A small barrel made of French oak for aging wine; imparts a particular flavor to the wine.

Bianco
White.

Bottiglia
Bottle.

Bricco
Term in the Piedmont for a vineyard at the top of a hill.

Cantina
Winery or commercial cellar.

Cantina sociale
Cooperative winery where grape growers pool their grapes to be made into wine.

Classico
A historic area with specified boundaries within a larger zone (for example, Chianti Classico or Soave Classico), as well as the wine from that area, which is, generally, although not always, considered to be better than other wines in the zone. In modern times, the boundaries have been expanded, as in Soave Classico, so "historic" is sometimes a relative term.

Clone
Genetically identical grapes selected and propagated from one "mother" vine, usually chosen for superior qualities according to local climate and conditions.

Colle
Hill.

Consorzio
An association of wine producers, usually authorized to make and enforce wine regulations and to promote the wines of its area.

DOC

Denominazione di Origine Controllata (Denomination of Controlled Origin), the foundation of Italian wine regulations, is essentially a set of rules establishing the official boundaries of various wine-producing regions. It also specifies which grapes can be used, limits the size of the harvest (to prevent overproduction, which could dilute quality), and sets up requirements for methods and timing of aging regimens. Tasting panels and testing programs intend to assure that the rules are followed. (The key word is "intend.")

Thus, DOCs are always geographically oriented, even when a grape-variety name is used. It is not, however, a guarantee of quality. The rules and regulations of DOCs are drawn up by grape growers, winemakers, and politicians and tend to be generous. They also tend to be revised, which can be an upward process, as in the case of the tightening of standards in Tuscany for Chianti Classico, or a downward one, as in the case of the loosening of standards in the Soave Classico zone. Still, it is a discipline, and has undoubtedly raised the overall quality of Italian wine.

DOCG

Denominazione di Origine Controllata e Garantita (Denomination of Controlled and Guaranteed Origin) is a step up from plain DOC, indicating a zone and wine of high and individual esteem (many DOCs include dozens of wine types within a specified area, and are drawn on political boundary lines, while DOCGs concentrate on special wines from historic, classic zones). Controls are more rigid than for DOCs, and most of these wines are of the highest quality possible. The key word here is "possible." Some are merely historic, made as well as they can be made, but are still not terribly exciting, as in the case of Emilia-Romagna's Albana. Happily, it's one of the few exceptions to the high standard. Aside from the designation on the label, all DOCG wines carry a paper-strip seal over the cork at the top of the bottle.

Dolce
Sweet.

Enoteca
Wine shop or wine bar, or sometimes a restaurant specializing in or famous for wine.

Etichetta
Label.

Fattoria
In the old days, a large estate whose vineyards were farmed by sharecroppers who contributed a portion of their grapes; still seen on labels, though the system has ended.

Fiasco
Flask.

Frizzante
Lightly bubbly, with just enough carbon dioxide to fizz on the tongue.

IGT

Indicazione Geografica Tipica (Typical Geographic Indication) is basically a category created to recognize modern Italian wines, either new blends of old grape varieties, such as the array of whites from Sicily combining Catarratto, Inzolia, and Grillo in varying proportions, or blends of old and new varieties, such as Antinori's famous and expensive Tignanello, which is a mix of Sangiovese, Cabernet Sauvignon, and Cabernet Franc. (Just to make it more interesting, in some regions, such as Friuli, long-established varieties like Chardonnay may be included in the DOC, while recently planted Cabernet Sauvignon may be classified as IGT.) Also included in this wide-ranging category are quality wines that deviate, for whatever reason, from the DOC procedures for winemaking, for example the amount of time the wines spend in oak barrels. IGT is, in the end, an ambiguous catch-all classification, certainly regulated and often containing wonderful wines, but with few real assurances beyond the name and reputation of the producer.

Imbottigliato all'origine
Estate bottled.

Imbottigliato da
Bottled by, usually followed by the name of the vintner or estate.

Invecchiato
Aged.

Masseria
A farm; most often used in southern Italy.

Metodo classico
Sparkling wine made in the classic (Champagne) method of fermenting the wine in a bottle; usually from high-quality grapes.

Normale
Standard; usually applied to the basic level of a category of wines.

Passito
Sweet wine made from semidried grapes, which concentrates the sugar and flavor.

Pergola
System of training vines to grow over elevated trellises or wires in a fan shape; also, a grape arbor.

Podere
In the old days, a small farm operated by a sharecropper; now a historic or sentimental name for an estate.

Profumo
Scent.

Recioto
Wine made from semidried grapes, often sweet but also sometimes dry, as in Amarone; most commonly used around Verona.

Riserva
Reserve, used to denote a wine in the DOC or DOCG category that has been aged for a specified time and in a specified way (for example, in oak barrels or in bottles) at the winery.

Ronco
Terraced hillside vineyard.

Rosato
Rosé wine.

Rosso
Red.

Secco
Dry.

Sori
A particularly sunny slope; used in the Piedmont to denote special vineyards, especially for Barolo and Barbaresco.

Spumante
Sparkling wine.

Superiore
A DOC wine of higher standard than the norm for the region, usually due to higher alcohol content (from riper grapes) or longer aging; not necessarily a guarantee of quality.

Tenuta
Estate or farm, mainly for wine.

Uva
Grape.

Uvaggio
A mixture of grape varieties.

VdT
Vino da Tavola (Table Wine) is a category that generally covers bulk wine sold to local restaurants or wine sold from one winery to another for blending. It is the lowest level of classification for the cheapest wines. Oddly, a decade ago some of Italy's most expensive wines, the so-called Super-Tuscans created from French grapes such as Cabernet Sauvignon and Merlot, also fell into this category, a catch-22 situation that eventually extended to similar "foreign" wines made in other regions. The problem was finally solved in Tuscany by creating a DOC specifically for some of the wines; in other regions, they're easily spotted by their high price tags.

Vecchio
Old.

Vendemmia
Grape harvest; the vintage year.

Zucchero
Sugar.

Italian Wine
and **Food**

Northwest : Piedmont, Valle d'Aosta, Liguria, Lombardy

Even in the fractured history of Italy's republics, kingdoms, principalities, and city-states, the Piedmont stands out, because for a long time it stood apart. For nearly a thousand years, it was a proud and prosperous royal outpost of France, which left culinary markers everywhere in the region. (The first Italian cookbook published in its capital, Turin, known as "the most Italian city of France," was subtitled "corrected in Paris.") Much of that interwoven tradition, combining elegance and heartiness, is still in evidence today.

Valle d'Aosta, to the north of the Piedmont, has its French angles, too. It was once owned by Burgundy and then annexed by the Piedmont, which co-opted its agricultural products, especially the rich cheese, butter, and cream from pampered cows that grazed on dense grass in high mountain valleys.

Liguria, a thin crescent of land to the south of the Piedmont, hidden behind a mountain range that crowds it toward the sea, made its fortune from the ships that sailed in and out of Genoa, still the largest port in Italy. Its cuisine, however, was shaped less by sailors and the sea than by as much sunshine as any farmer or gardener could ever hope to see.

Lombardy, conquered at various times by Germany, Spain, and Austria, and annexed by Venice and then by the Piedmont, shuffled and reshuffled the gastronomic cards it was given and came up with a cuisine based on butter and cream and slow cooking. It is neither an accident nor a surprise that one of the holiest of the world's temples of gastronomy, the incredibly luxurious delicatessen known as Peck's, was established in Lombardy's capital of Milan more than a hundred years ago.

A lot of Italy's gastronomic glory has long come from the northwest: mushrooms and white truffles from the Piedmont, pesto and other uplifting herb concoctions from Liguria, Fontina and other luscious cheeses from Valle d'Aosta and Lombardy, rice for risotto from the length of the Po River valley, and the inventive cooking of cosmopolitan Milan.

Mountains define the landscape of these wine regions, from the long arc of the Alps along their northern edge, to the southern side, where the Apennine chain cordons off Liguria and begins its long journey down the length of the Italian boot. Even in the fertile plains of the Po River valley, mountains give the horizon a jagged shape. On the hills, vineyards seem to tumble recklessly down steep slopes. The phrase "as the crow flies" is meaningless here, where it might take you forty-five minutes to drive to the nearest hilltop: down a slanting road of S bends, along a flat riverside stretch until you find a bridge, then back and up another snaking road, all the while wondering how anyone farms these steep, straight rows of vines (*a mano*, they'll tell you, "by hand"). The leading grape of the area is Nebbiolo, named for the fog (*nebbia*) trapped between the hills most mornings. When the sun comes out and you see a rainbow rising out of a deep valley and soaring over the peaks before disappearing down into another valley, it's a heart-stopping sight.

Several of the Piedmont's wines are Italy's noblest, while others are evolving dynamically. To the north and south, the

steep terraces of Liguria and Valle d'Aosta demand a dedica-
tion bordering on the heroic, and winemakers are just holding
their own, although their best efforts are worth seeking out.
The industrial prosperity of Milan and Lombardy has crowded
out many vineyards, but a few distinctive table wines and
several classic sparkling wines still testify to a once-grand
tradition. More important, that prosperity (and, sometimes,
the need to display it) creates a thriving market for quality
wine, helping to raise the standards, and also contributes to
the wine revival elsewhere. Many owners of newly ambitious
vineyard estates in Tuscany, Umbria, and the south are
wealthy northerners who have bought into what hardworking
locals wryly refer to as "the glamor of wine."

Red Wines

Barolo and Barbaresco

Barolo and Barbaresco are two of Italy's greatest red wines, made exclusively from Nebbiolo grapes, expensive and highly prized, greatly esteemed around the world for centuries. (Thomas Jefferson, America's first international wine lover, was a fan of Barolo more than two hundred years ago, and he was joined by a long line of European nobility.) Barolo has long been known as "the king of wines, the wine of kings," while Barbaresco, grown in a neighboring zone, has also been considered noble, but a slightly junior partner—more of a crown prince, perhaps. It's an unfair comparison, and now fading.

The reputation of Barolo and Barbaresco came from their rare combination of power and elegance, and the fact that, although they are made from one type of grape and not a blend, they gain remarkable complexity of taste and aroma, as well as silky-smooth texture, when they age. Amazingly, some fairly ordinary wines are made from the Nebbiolo grape, which proves that, for vineyards, location matters. Nebbiolo only reaches its full, noble potential on the steep slopes of the Barolo and Barbaresco districts that give the wine its name: the combination of well-drained gravelly hillsides, prevailing morning fog that acts as an air-conditioner, and clear afternoon mountain sunshine boost the grape to its full potential here.

The differences between the two wines are not considerable. Barbaresco is a marginally warmer district, and so the wines are slightly lighter, although that's relative, as they're still wines on a grand scale. Both are hard and tightly tannic when young, basically full bodied and robust, needing about ten years after the vintage to come around to mellow maturity. When they evolve into that grown-up stage, they provide an abundance of persistent and lingering aromas of dried flowers, a flash of earthiness, and an intriguing characteristic scent of tar and roses.

TYPICAL AROMAS AND FLAVORS
The more noble the wine, the more aromas and flavors we perceive. Here, it's an abundance that may include tar, roses, plums, tobacco, violets, cloves, and leather, with occasional hints of vanilla, dried flowers, and cherry liqueur.

TIPS TO SUCCESSFUL MATCHES
WITH BAROLO AND BARBARESCO
- *These are big wines, so they need big food. Rich, deep flavors are the best, like those found in pot roast, beef stew, casseroles of meat and root vegetables, and braised lamb shanks or venison.*
- *The high acidity that helps these wines age well also cuts right through rich, dense sauces and gravies.*
- *The Piedmont is truffle country, and there's a neighborhood compatibility of Barolo and Barbaresco with those wonderfully funky fungi, as well as with mushrooms. Try a rare grilled steak smothered with glazed mushrooms and see.*

Barbera

Barbera was Italy's workhorse grape for a long time, planted and thriving all around the country (and in North and South America, thanks to Italian immigrants) and prized for contributing color and acidity to blends with other grapes and wines, but almost never in the spotlight on its own. Then, in 1982, Giacomo Bologna, an ebullient winemaker in the Piedmont, got the idea of aging his Barbera in small barrels of French oak (known as *barriques*), which raised the level of tannin, toned down the acidity, and added some spice to its aroma. A star was born. Barbera quickly became a Cinderella wine, as most other winemakers in the area adopted the techniques. (It's appropriate that the transformation took place where it did, as the Piedmont is probably where the grape originated.)

This is a full-bodied wine, often even voluptuous, but not ponderous or heavy. Its signature lively streak of acidity keeps it buoyant, and its ample bouquet is welcoming. The firm tannin and relatively high alcohol insure its potential to age well, with an average target date of about five years after the vintage for the best flavor, although some single-vineyard versions easily hold up well for a decade.

The Barbera grape is grown throughout Italy, but lends its name to the wine in three principal areas, all in the Piedmont: Barbera d'Alba is generally considered to set the standard, pretty much the baseline wine, while Barbera d'Asti is usually slightly lighter. Barbera del Monferrato comes from a large area and varies in style from light to dense, but at least there's a family resemblance. Wines labeled with these basic appellations are the mainstream. Up a notch in strength, muscular tannins, oak flavors, and definitely price are the single-vineyard bottlings or wines with brand names, such as Bologna's Bricco dell'Uccelone or Chiarlo's La Court. They're serious wines, and age worthy, meant to be drunk years after the vintage.

TYPICAL AROMAS AND FLAVORS

Plums, blackberry jam, and the tartness of wild cherry are characteristic, with hints sometimes of mixed spices, licorice, and coffee.

TIPS TO SUCCESSFUL MATCHES WITH BARBERA

- *Hot and spicy dishes often clash with alcohol and oak, so they don't make a good match with Barbera.*
- *Choose dishes with full-flavored sauces to complement the rich mellowness of the wine.*
- *Barbera's lively mixed-berry aromas and acidity make it a good companion to barbecued and grilled meats, especially sausages, spareribs, and even burgers.*

Dolcetto

The name in Italian means "the little sweet one,"
an affectionate tribute to the way the relatively low-
acid Dolcetto ripens easily up in the cool hills where
other grapes often struggle, and also to the amiable,
uncomplicated nature of the wine. This is the everyday,
easygoing wine of the Piedmont, deeply purple, basically soft and lush, jam-packed with flavor. Dolcetto
can even be pleasant when lightly chilled (half an
hour in the fridge is about right), so it's also a good
summer wine.

Basically, this is a wine to drink young, between
one and two years after the vintage, when its luscious,
round character is at its peak. Cheerful, informal
occasions and meals suit Dolcetto best, as its unique
combination of lightness and mellowness enables it to
match well with a variety of different, and sometimes
offbeat, foods. It's one of the few reds that can match
quiche, steak tartare, or *salade niçoise*, for example,
and it's positively made in heaven alongside pasta
tossed with a cheese sauce.

Besides simple Dolcettos, there are seven different
appellations whose names are attached to the grape.
Alba, Diano d'Alba, and Dogliani are considered to be
the consistently best quality, by a small margin.

TYPICAL AROMAS AND FLAVORS
*Predominantly mulberry, with overtones of raspberry
and musk, and hints of almond, sometimes mint,
and candied fruit.*

TIPS TO SUCCESSFUL MATCHES
WITH DOLCETTO

- *A rich fruitiness and softness make Dolcetto a good wine
  for cross-cultural matches, especially hot and spicy foods.*
- *It's also a good crossover wine; that is, the sort of red
  wine that partners equally well with white meat like
  chicken, turkey, or pork, especially if they're grilled or in
  a tomato-based sauce, and simple veal dishes.*
- *The wine's considerable berryish fruitiness contrasts
  nicely with salty and savory foods, making it a flexible
  partner for antipasto platters featuring salami, prosciutto,
  and other kinds of ham, cheese, and even nuts.*

Gattinara and Ghemme

In the high hills in the north of the Piedmont, the growing season can be short and cool. The wines made from the Nebbiolo grapes that grow around the towns of Gattinara and Ghemme are usually lighter and a shade more tart than their noble siblings, the full-flavored Barolos and Barbarescos that flourish to the south. They are relatively rare and something of a curiosity, but in the warm second half of the 1990s, when the Piedmont saw a string of good vintages, Gattinara and Ghemme began to come into their own as interesting, aromatic junior versions of fine wines, worth trying if you run across them.

TYPICAL AROMAS AND FLAVORS
Certainly plums, with a touch of licorice and violets, and a faint hint of coffee.

TIP TO SUCCESSFUL MATCHES
WITH GATTINARA AND GHEMME
- *The wines are slightly rustic, with a mildly bitter aftertaste that suits game and full-flavored meats, such as venison, wild rabbit, pheasant, wild boar, or lamb, especially if they're marinated or cooked with strong sauces.*

Freisa

Freisa is an oddity, worth noting because it's making a small comeback. It's also unique: the color is garnet, the body is fairly light, and the very fruity taste is distinctly and deliciously of raspberries. Some versions are even slightly sparkling, delivering just a little bit of fizz on your tongue. It's more of a wine for fun than thinking about: very refreshing, best lightly chilled, perfect on its own or with light snacks and appetizers.

White Wines

Gavi

Gavi is a pretty good, often very good, wine that is sometimes a victim of its success, pushed around a bit by marketing hype. As a dry wine of any distinction, it's pretty much a modern phenomenon. The vineyards are more than one thousand years old, but the wines were usually blended anonymously until the mid-twentieth century, when a successful marketing campaign made Gavi a star, and an expensive one besides, under the name Gavi dei Gavi. It made the wine seem like the best of the best, when actually the name was much like saying San Francisco of San Francisco.

The grape is actually Cortese, and since the wine is good enough to have remained fashionable, the name game has continued. Today, you might see Gavi di Gavi, Cortese di Gavi, Gavi-and-a-fancy-name, and, once in a great while, just plain Gavi. Whatever it's called, it's always worth a try. Gavi is lightly scented, thoroughly dry, and blessed with tingling, crisp acidity—refreshing and a little sturdier than many Italian whites. Though only medium bodied, it somehow feels more substantial. It's a bit too dry and subtle to be a good sipping wine or aperitif, but it comes into its own with food.

TYPICAL AROMAS AND FLAVORS

Apple and peach are the most common flavor and aroma associations, with hints of flint or clean, fresh stone in the aftertaste, and sometimes tangerine.

TIPS TO SUCCESSFUL MATCHES WITH GAVI

- *The subtlety of the wine's aroma is an advantage when it comes to matching it with dishes cooked with herbs or spices—the wine doesn't compete, but supports the food terrifically.*
- *Gavi's firm acidity makes it a perfect match with rich fish stews and full-flavored shellfish dishes. If you like white wine with cioppino, Gavi is the one, and it's a great mate to spaghetti with clams in a parsley-garlic sauce.*

Arneis

Twenty years ago, I pulled off a gastronomic hat trick: three meals in two days at La Contea, a small restaurant in the tiny Piedmontese hamlet of Neive that continues to be considered one of Italy's best. I can still remember every dish, but one wine stands out among the fantastic Barolos and Barbarescos I was tasting. Bruno Ceretto, one of the pioneers of modern winemaking in the Piedmont, poured out a white wine from a bottle with no label and asked my opinion, which was a little like Marlon Brando asking for my theories on acting. I'd never smelled or tasted anything quite like it: The aroma was floral, but I couldn't pin down the flowers, and there were fleeting hints of other familiar and pleasant smells, while the taste was like first-rate unsweetened fruit salad, definite but impossible to pick apart. As if that weren't bad enough, there was a slight flavor of toasted almonds in the aftertaste.

I was stumped. Intrigued? Absolutely. Confused? Definitely. Bruno told me the wine was from a grape called Arneis, which in the local dialect meant "stubborn rascal," because it was hard to grow (or maybe, he added ruefully, the name should apply to those who grew it). It was an ancient variety, and he and a few of his neighbors had decided it was worth reviving. Arneis, from vineyards around the town of Roero, has become a deservedly popular wine, in Italy and abroad. Like all aromatic wines, it should be drunk young, when it's freshest.

TIP TO SUCCESSFUL MATCHES WITH ARNEIS
- *Its distinctive and complicated yet subtle aromas mean it goes best with relatively simple food, especially appetizers, and pasta combined with cheese or seafood, such as squid or octopus.*

Asti Spumante

Asti Spumante is a light, fairly sweet sparkling wine made from the Moscato Bianco (White Muscat) grape, rarely taken seriously by wine snobs, but one of Italy's most popular wines around the world. In some countries, it outsells Champagne. It is always worth at least a sip (though not necessarily at a wedding or other large social occasion where the host may have economized on the wine). The taste can be surprisingly good, as this is the sort of wine that has benefited from the clean, controlled conditions modern technology has brought to winemaking.

It's a bulk-process wine, usually made in large stainless-steel tanks in fairly large quantities, relatively low in alcohol (rarely more than 12 percent, often less), shipped right off to market when young and fresh, generally inexpensive, and while not at all serious, often refreshing and fun. The Muscat grape has a somewhat musky aroma and flavor that gives the wine a nice extra dimension, slightly spicy, and the best examples actually skip nimbly along a line that's neither too dry nor too sweet. This successful straddle makes them welcome at either end of a meal, as good aperitifs with simple nibbles, or after dinner with fruit tarts or compotes or even creamy mild cheeses.

TYPICAL AROMAS AND FLAVORS
A light mix of peaches and pears, with a hint of musk.

TIP TO SUCCESSFUL MATCHES WITH ASTI SPUMANTE
- *The sweetness level of the food is the most important thing. It can be less than that of the wine, but never more, or it simply knocks out the pleasure of the pairing. Cheese straws and toasted almonds are fine, as are shortbread cookies or poached pears.*

Moscato d'Asti

Made from the same grape as Asti Spumante, but with less alcohol (5 or 6 percent), fewer bubbles (fizzy rather than sparkling), and more musky spice, these wines are still a rarity but gaining popularity. They have a smooth, creamy texture and are made in a range of styles, from slightly sweet to sweet, but the export versions are mainly on the sweeter side. In the Piedmont, people often have a glass of Moscato d'Asti at the end of a large meal, on its own, just for sheer pleasurable refreshment. On the other hand, the big surprise is that, contrary to all expectations for a white wine, it goes well with chocolate.

Vermouth

If your fate is to be drowned in martinis, then you can't expect much respect, and thanks to gin, vodka, and James Bond, that's what happened to Vermouth. Once considered a noble beverage, Vermouth still commands respect in the wine regions of western Europe. If you go to the gloriously baroque cut-glass-and-gilt Caffè Confetteria al Bicerin, on the Piazza della Consolata in Turin, you can choose from among a whole array of white and red Vermouths, plain or as the main ingredient in various light drinks, just as Alexandre Dumas, Puccini, Nietzsche, and thousands of others have done since 1786, when the wine was invented nearby (the *caffè* actually dates from 1736). It's certainly the right place to discover that Vermouth can be a very nice drink.

Vermouth is concocted by blending wine with secret combinations of herbs, spices, and other natural flavorings that have been steeped in small amounts of brandy to bring out their essences. There are hundreds of flavored wines made in Europe, originally for reasons of health and good digestion, and Vermouth is the most enduring and popular. The red version tends to be somewhat sweet (though still with a herbal aspect), the white version quite dry. In the summer, I like to drink the sweet type over ice, topped up with about one-fourth sparkling lemonade and a lemon twist and balanced by a dash of bitter Campari, or a half-and-half blend of the sweet and dry over ice with a twist. Either goes well with salted peanuts or almonds.

Northwest : Recipes

Pasta with Potatoes, Green Beans, and Pesto

RECOMMENDED WINE: **Gavi**
ALTERNATIVE WINE: **Arneis**

Is this a pasta dish or a vegetable dish? In Liguria, where my wife and I used to eat this as a first course most evenings at our favorite outdoor restaurant on the beach, it never seemed to matter—it's just a sexy traditional dish there. Back home, we often have it alone as a simple lunch, while for dinner we serve it with grilled fish, and some crisp light white wine.

1 pound dried fettuccine

2 waxy potatoes, peeled and
  cut into ½-inch dice

8 ounces green beans, trimmed
  and cut in half crosswise

½ cup Pesto (page 196)

SERVES 4 AS A MAIN COURSE

BRING A LARGE POT FILLED WITH WATER TO A BOIL. Snap the fettuccine in half and add to the boiling water along with the potatoes. Cook until the pasta is al dente and the potatoes are tender, about 11 minutes. Meanwhile, in another pan of boiling water, cook the beans until tender, about 4 minutes.

DRAIN THE POTATO-PASTA MIX GENTLY, reserving a bit of the cooking water, and place in a large bowl. Drain the beans and add to the bowl. Mix 2 tablespoons of the cooking water with the Pesto, add to the bowl, and toss the mixture lightly until coated with the sauce. Serve at once.

Spinach Gnocchi
with Cheese Sauce

RECOMMENDED WINE: **Dolcetto**

ALTERNATIVE WINE: **Gattinara or Ghemme**

Semolina flour is made from durum wheat, the basis for most good pasta, and can also be fashioned into these tasty spinach dumplings, here topped with a rich cheese sauce. The addition of a couple of grilled sausages on the side rounds out a very good meal. My first choice for wine would be a good light red, but the dish is quite comfortable with white, too.

1 pound spinach, well rinsed and
  tough stems removed

2 large eggs, lightly beaten

1/2 cup grated Parmesan cheese

1 tablespoon chopped fresh sage

pinch of salt

1/4 teaspoon freshly ground black pepper

2 cups milk

2 tablespoons unsalted butter

1 1/2 cups semolina flour

SAUCE:

2 tablespoons unsalted butter

2 tablespoons all-purpose flour

2 cups milk

1/4 teaspoon freshly grated nutmeg

salt

3/4 cup grated Parmesan cheese

SERVES 6

PUT THE SPINACH, with just the rinsing water clinging to the leaves, in a saucepan, cover, place over medium heat, and cook just until wilted, about 2 minutes. Drain in a sieve, rinse under cold water to cool, and squeeze dry. Chop roughly. Place the spinach in a blender or food processor with the eggs, cheese, sage, salt, and pepper. Pulse a few times, just enough to chop the spinach further and completely mix in the other ingredients.

IN A LARGE HEAVY-BOTTOMED SAUCEPAN, bring the milk to a steady simmer over medium heat. Melt the butter into the milk and then sprinkle in the semolina in a steady stream, stirring all the while to prevent lumps from forming. It will thicken quickly, but keep stirring until it is cooked, about 10 minutes. It will come away from the sides of the pan when it is done.

REMOVE FROM THE HEAT, add the spinach mixture and stir vigorously. Pour onto 1 or 2 lightly oiled rimmed baking sheets. The semolina mixture should be about 1/2 inch deep. Refrigerate until cool and set, about 1 hour.

PREHEAT THE OVEN TO 425°F.

LIGHTLY OIL A LARGE BAKING DISH. To make the gnocchi, use a water glass or a cookie cutter to cut out rounds about 2 inches in diameter. Or shape the gnocchi by scooping out 1 heaping tablespoon at a time and patting it into shape (keep your hands moistened with water to prevent sticking). Place the gnocchi in the baking dish in a single layer, overlapping them slightly.

TO MAKE THE SAUCE, in a heavy-bottomed saucepan melt the butter over low heat. Add the flour and cook, stirring, until the mixture forms a paste and is bubbly, about 2 minutes. Slowly pour in the milk while stirring constantly. Continue cooking, stirring constantly, until the sauce thickens, about 5 minutes. Remove from the heat, season with the nutmeg and salt to taste, and stir in 1/2 cup of the cheese.

POUR THE SAUCE OVER THE GNOCCHI. Sprinkle the remaining cheese evenly over the top. Bake the gnocchi until the top begins to brown, about 20 minutes. Serve hot.

Pasta with Chicken, Spinach, and Herb Sauce, North Beach Style

RECOMMENDED WINE: Barbera d'Alba

ALTERNATIVE WINE: Dolcetto

Thirty years ago, among us bohemians at least, it was the custom to eat family style in San Francisco's North Beach, sharing tables, so-so wine, bad jokes, and steaming bowls of garlicky abundance with whomever else had been lucky enough to elbow their way in and snag a chair or part of a bench. At Caffè Sport, Capp's Corner, New Pisa, Gold Spike, and La Pantera, locals and tourists alike tucked into old-fashioned Italian home cooking (and cioppino on Friday nights), and no one was too sophisticated to have a good time. This recipe reminds me of those good old days. It's from Cucina Viansa, the restaurant on the square in Sonoma, California, owned by Sam and Vicky Sebastiani, who created the Viansa Winery in Carneros in 1988, and still have an ideal of blending the best of California and Italy. Serve it with plenty of sourdough bread for mopping up the delicious sauce.

TOMATO SAUCE:

3 tablespoons olive oil

1 onion, chopped

1 carrot, peeled and chopped

1 celery stalk, chopped

2 tablespoons chopped fresh parsley

1 clove garlic, chopped

2 cups chopped, peeled tomatoes

1 cup boiling water

4 boneless, skinless chicken breast halves

4 tablespoons olive oil

1/4 teaspoon salt, plus more to taste

1/4 teaspoon freshly ground black pepper,
   plus more to taste

6 ounces fresh cremini or shiitake mushrooms, sliced

2 tablespoons minced garlic

2 tablespoons minced fresh thyme

1/2 cup reduced-sodium canned chicken broth

12 ounces penne

8 ounces spinach, well rinsed, tough stems removed,
   and leaves roughly chopped if large

1/2 cup mixed chopped fresh basil, tarragon,
   chervil, chives, and parsley (1 heaping tablespoon each)

1 cup grated Parmesan cheese

1/2 cup ricotta cheese

SERVES 6 AS A MAIN COURSE

TO MAKE THE SAUCE, in a heavy-bottomed saucepan, heat the olive oil over medium heat. Add the onion, carrot, celery, parsley, and garlic and cook, stirring, until the aroma rises and the vegetables soften, about 5 minutes. Add the tomatoes and boiling water, bring to a boil, cover, reduce the heat to medium, and simmer for 30 minutes. Remove the cover and simmer for 15 minutes longer to reduce the sauce. Remove from the heat and let cool. Push through a sieve or a food mill into a bowl. Set aside.

LIGHT A FIRE IN A CHARCOAL GRILL OR PREHEAT THE BROILER. Toss the chicken with 2 tablespoons of the olive oil and ¼ teaspoon each salt and pepper until evenly coated. Place the chicken breasts on the grill rack or on a broiler pan and grill or broil 4 inches from the heat source until half-cooked, about 5 minutes on each side. Remove from the grill or broiler, cut into bite-sized pieces, and set aside.

IN A LARGE HEAVY-BOTTOMED SAUCEPAN, heat the remaining 2 tablespoons olive oil over medium-high heat. Add the mushrooms and sauté until they release their moisture, about 4 minutes. Add the garlic and thyme and cook for 2 minutes. Add the broth and the tomato sauce. As soon as the sauce comes to an active simmer, reduce the heat to medium-low and cook, uncovered, to reduce slightly and to blend the flavors, about 10 minutes. Add the chicken to the sauce and cook until opaque throughout, about 10 minutes.

WHILE THE SAUCE IS COOKING, bring a large pot filled with salted water to a boil. Add the pasta, stir well, and cook until al dente, about 11 minutes. Drain.

ADD THE PASTA AND SPINACH TO THE SAUCE AND STIR WELL. Taste and adjust the seasoning with salt and pepper. Remove from the heat and add the herbs and half of the Parmesan cheese. Stir well.

TO SERVE, divide among warmed bowls and top with dollops of the ricotta. Pass the rest of the Parmesan at the table.

Prawn, Red Pepper, and Leek **Risotto**

RECOMMENDED WINE: **Gavi**

ALTERNATIVE WINE: **Arneis**

Prawns are naturally sweet, and so are ripe peppers, and leeks get that way when cooked. Put them all together and they make a nice, natural fit. Add tarragon (in Italian, a very operatic *dragoncello*) and it's heavenly. This risotto should be a little bit wet, as the texture enhances the flavor, so don't let it dry out. The prawns are added at the end to keep them from overcooking, but using the shells in the stock insures that their flavor comes through. The finished dish is so fresh and mellow that it goes well with a variety of easygoing whites.

8 ounces tiger prawns

1 cup water

6 cups reduced-sodium canned chicken broth

1 tablespoon unsalted butter

2 tablespoons olive oil

3 leeks, white part only, chopped

2 red bell peppers, seeded, deribbed,
  and cut into 1/4-inch dice

2 cups Arborio rice

1 1/2 tablespoons chopped fresh tarragon

1 cup dry white wine

2 tablespoons minced fresh chives

SERVES 4 AS A MAIN COURSE

PEEL AND DEVEIN THE PRAWNS, reserving the shells. Place the prawns in a bowl of cold water to cover and refrigerate. In a saucepan, combine the shells and 1 cup water over medium heat. Bring to a simmer and cook for 5 minutes; the shells will turn pink. Strain the liquid and discard the shells. Return the liquid to the saucepan, add the broth, and bring to a bare simmer.

IN A HEAVY-BOTTOMED SAUCEPAN, melt the butter with the olive oil over low heat. Add the leeks and bell peppers and cook until soft, about 5 minutes. Increase the heat to medium, and add the rice and tarragon to the pan. Stir vigorously to coat all the grains with the fat, and cook, stirring, until opaque, 2 to 3 minutes. Add the wine and cook, stirring, until nearly absorbed. Add about 1/2 cup of the broth and cook, stirring frequently, until absorbed. Continue adding the broth, 1/2 cup at a time and waiting until it is absorbed before adding more. Stir gently and often to keep the rice from sticking.

WHEN THE RICE IS NEARLY DONE, after a total of about 20 minutes, drain the prawns, cut them in half crosswise, and add them to the pan. Stir gently until the prawns turn pink and are opaque throughout, about 4 minutes. The rice is ready when the grains are tender but slightly firm in the center and the mixture is creamy. If it is not ready, cook for another 2 minutes or so. If it is still firm and you have no more stock, add 1/2 cup hot water and cook until absorbed.

DIVIDE THE RISOTTO EVENLY AMONG WARMED SHALLOW BOWLS, garnish with the chives, and serve at once.

Pan-Roasted **Veal Tenderloin** with Mushrooms, Fingerling Potatoes, Prosciutto, and Truffle Oil

RECOMMENDED WINE: **Barolo**

ALTERNATIVE WINE: **Barbaresco**

Chef-owner Arnold Eric Wong and his partner Debbie Zachereas of San Francisco's Bacar restaurant have assembled one of the best wine lists I've ever seen, and they reinforce their commitment to wine by creating winemakers' dinners, tailoring the dishes to specific wines. This dish was part of a fabulous dinner built around the Piedmontese wines of Angelo Gaja, one of the world's great winemakers. Arnold said he wanted to make a dish that would complement the wine without getting in its way—a good accompanist.

6 to 8 fingerling potatoes of uniform size, unpeeled

4 leeks, white part only, cut crosswise into
 ¾-inch lengths

1 veal tenderloin, about 14 ounces

salt and freshly ground black pepper

2 tablespoons grapeseed or sunflower oil

1 tablespoon olive oil

6 ounces fresh hen-of-the-woods, shiitake, or
 cremini mushrooms, cut into ¼-inch strips

3 slices prosciutto, cut into narrow strips

½ cup dry red wine

½ cup veal or chicken stock

2 tablespoons truffle oil

SERVES 2

PREHEAT THE OVEN TO 400°F.

PLACE THE POTATOES IN A SAUCEPAN AND ADD LIGHTLY SALTED WATER TO COVER. Bring to a boil and cook, uncovered, until tender when pierced with a knife tip, 15 to 20 minutes. Drain and let cool. Cut lengthwise in half and set aside. Refill the saucepan with lightly salted water and bring to a boil over high heat. Add the leeks, blanch for 30 seconds, and drain. Immediately place them in a bowl of very cold water until cool. Drain again and set aside.

CUT THE VEAL TENDERLOIN INTO 1 ½-INCH-THICK MEDALLIONS. Season with salt and pepper. In a sauté pan or skillet, heat the grapeseed oil over high heat. When very hot, add the medallions and sear, turning once, for about 2 minutes on each side. Transfer to a roasting pan, arranging them in a single layer, place in the oven, and roast until medium-rare, 3 to 4 minutes.

WHILE THE VEAL IS ROASTING, prepare the vegetables. In a heavy-bottomed sauté pan, heat the olive oil over medium heat. Add the mushrooms, leeks, and potatoes and cook, stirring occasionally, until the vegetables begin to color, about 5 minutes. Add the prosciutto, stir well, and season to taste with salt and pepper. Remove pan from heat and cover.

WHEN THE VEAL IS READY, transfer it to a warmed plate, cover loosely with aluminum foil, and let rest while you make the pan sauce. Place the roasting pan over high heat and add the wine and stock. Cook until reduced by half, 6 to 7 minutes.

TO SERVE, divide the potatoes, mushrooms, and leeks evenly between 2 warmed plates, arranging them to one side. Ladle half the pan sauce onto the other side of each plate. Place the veal medallions on top of the sauce and drizzle 1 tablespoon of truffle oil over each portion. Serve at once.

Rack of Lamb Roasted with Walnut-Pesto Crust

RECOMMENDED WINE: **Barolo**
ALTERNATIVE WINE: **Barbaresco**

The flavor of lamb is wonderful on its own, but it's vivid enough to carry many other strong flavors. I found this out when I tried alternatives to French and English ideas that use garlic or mustard, and discovered the delicious synergy between lamb and basil. Only the best, most full-flavored red wine will do.

4 racks of lamb, with 4 ribs each
salt and freshly ground black pepper
2 tablespoons sunflower oil
⅓ cup Pesto (page 196)
¼ cup walnuts, finely chopped
2 tablespoons olive oil
¼ cup dry white wine

SERVES 4

HAVE THE BUTCHER REMOVE THE CHINE BONE FROM THE RACKS, which will make browning and carving them easier. Trim the layer of fat off the top of the lamb. Season the meat lightly with salt and pepper.

IN A LARGE HEAVY-BOTTOMED SKILLET, heat the sunflower oil over medium-high heat. Add the lamb and sear the meat all over until well browned, 5 to 6 minutes total. Remove to a wire rack and let cool.

PREHEAT OVEN TO 450°F.

IN A SMALL BOWL, stir together the Pesto and walnuts, mixing well. Spread about 2 tablespoons of the mixture across the top (the meaty portion) of each rack. Place the racks in a large roasting pan.

ROAST THE LAMB FOR 5 MINUTES. Drizzle the olive oil evenly over the meat. Roast for 10 minutes longer for medium-rare.

REMOVE THE PAN FROM THE OVEN. Transfer the meat to a warmed plate, cover loosely with aluminum foil, and let rest for 5 minutes. Place the roasting pan over high heat on the stove top, pour in the wine, and bring to a boil, scraping the pan bottom with a wooden spoon to loosen the browned bits. Boil until reduced by half, 3 to 4 minutes.

TO SERVE, carve the lamb racks into chops and arrange on warmed plates. Drizzle the pan sauce over the chops and serve.

NOTE: *The lamb can be partially cooked in advance, making this one of the easiest elegant dinners possible. Brown the meat, let cool, and spread the Pesto on top as directed. Transfer to a covered dish and place in the refrigerator for up to 2 hours. About 20 minutes before cooking, while the oven preheats, remove the meat from the refrigerator to allow it to come to room temperature, then finish in the oven.*

Chicken and Portobello Mushrooms
Oven-Braised in Barbera

RECOMMENDED WINE: **Barbera d'Alba**
ALTERNATIVE WINE: **Barbera d'Asti**

Italians are more likely to have red wine than white with chicken, and a good choice for both cooking and drinking is Barbera, which is low in tannin but high in acidity, with a touch of red-cherry fruitiness. It's a red wine for white-wine drinkers, who will appreciate its zip and liveliness. Barberas from vineyards around the town of Alba tend to be a little richer than those from near Asti, farther north, but the Asti versions can be more vibrant. In the Piedmont, local cooks would serve a dish like this with polenta, but I think mashed potatoes sprinkled with chopped parsley are preferable, as they are lighter and soak up the juices better.

3 tablespoons olive oil

3 slices bacon, chopped

12 shallots, peeled but left whole

2 fresh portobello mushrooms, cut in half
   through the stem and then each half cut
   vertically into 1/4-inch-thick pieces

1 chicken, about 4 pounds, cut into serving pieces

1/4 cup all-purpose flour for dredging,
   plus 1 tablespoon

1 tablespoon dried thyme

salt and freshly ground black pepper

1 clove garlic, chopped

1 1/2 cups Barbera

1 cup reduced-sodium canned chicken broth

1 tablespoon unsalted butter

SERVES 4

PREHEAT THE OVEN TO 300°F.

IN A DUTCH OVEN OR OTHER HEAVY POT LARGE ENOUGH TO HOLD THE CHICKEN, heat the olive oil over medium heat. Add the bacon, shallots, and mushrooms and cook, stirring occasionally, until lightly browned, about 10 minutes. Using a slotted spoon, transfer the mix to a plate and set aside. Do not drain the pot.

RINSE THE CHICKEN PIECES AND PAT DRY. Place the 1/4 cup flour in a shallow bowl and season with the thyme, salt, and pepper. One at a time, roll the chicken pieces in the flour, shaking off the excess. Return the pot to medium heat and, working in batches if necessary, brown the chicken pieces on all sides. Add the garlic, bacon mixture, wine, and broth and bring to a simmer. Cover, place in the oven, and cook until the chicken is tender, about 1 1/2 hours.

IN A SMALL BOWL, work together the cold butter and 1 tablespoon flour into a lump. Cut it into 6 equal pieces. Remove the pot from the oven and, using a slotted spoon, remove the chicken to a plate. Place the pot over medium heat and bring the sauce to a simmer. Drop the butter-flour pieces into the pan juices one at a time, stirring well after each addition, then cook, stirring occasionally, until the juices thicken, about 5 minutes.

RETURN THE CHICKEN TO THE POT, cover, and braise over medium heat for 10 more minutes. Serve at once.

Chicken Liver **Risotto**

RECOMMENDED WINE: **Barbera d'Alba**
ALTERNATIVE WINE: **Dolcetto**

Risotto is something of a chameleon, changing dramatically as it absorbs flavors. It always amazes me how many incarnations are possible. Here is a good example, a simple but hearty and flavorful risotto, one of my favorite Sunday dinners in winter. It's also one of the most (red) wine-compatible dishes there is.

7 cups reduced-sodium canned chicken broth

1 tablespoon unsalted butter

2 tablespoons olive oil

1 onion, chopped

1 pound chicken livers

2 cups Arborio rice

4 ounces fresh white mushrooms, chopped

1 cup dry white wine

¼ cup grated Parmesan cheese

2 tablespoons chopped fresh parsley

SERVES 4 AS A MAIN COURSE

POUR THE CHICKEN BROTH INTO A SAUCEPAN AND BRING TO A SIMMER ON A BACK BURNER. Adjust the heat to maintain a bare simmer. In a heavy-bottomed saucepan, melt the butter with the olive oil over low heat. Add the onion and cook, stirring occasionally, until softened but not browned, about 5 minutes. Carefully add the chicken livers and brown them all over, but do not cook them through. Using a slotted spoon, transfer the chicken livers to a plate and set aside.

INCREASE THE HEAT TO MEDIUM AND ADD THE RICE TO THE PAN. Stir vigorously to coat all the grains with the fat and cook, stirring, until opaque, 2 to 3 minutes. Add the mushrooms and the wine and cook, stirring, until the wine is nearly absorbed. Add about ½ cup of the broth and cook, stirring frequently, until absorbed. Continue adding the broth, ½ cup at a time and waiting until it is absorbed before adding more. Stir gently and often to keep the rice from sticking. When the rice is nearly done, after a total of about 20 minutes, cut the chicken livers in half and return them to the pan. Stir gently for a few minutes, add the cheese, and then stir again. The rice is ready when the grains are tender but slightly firm in the center and the mixture is creamy. If it is not ready, cook for another 2 minutes or so. If it is still firm and you have no more stock, add ½ cup hot water and cook until absorbed.

DIVIDE THE RISOTTO EVENLY AMONG WARMED SHALLOW BOWLS, garnish with the parsley, and serve at once.

Northeast : Veneto, Trentino–Alto Adige, Friuli–Venezia Giulia

Together, these three northeast regions are known as the Tre Venezie. They were once part of the great Republic of Venice in political but not cultural alliances, a situation that continues in many ways today. Alto Adige used to be the South Tirol, part of Austria until after World War I, and it remains resolutely Teutonic. The best part of that equation is the area's elegant white wines, some of Italy's best. Trentino looks more to the Veneto for inspiration and holds a middle ground for food, high ground for wines. Friuli–Venezia Giulia is a similar awkward political entity. Its eastern edge is another post–World War I annexation (mainly to get custody of Trieste), but the fact that it was both a frontier and a highway for conquering armies for thousands of years left it with a rich, tangled legacy, reflected today in unique, deliciously elevated peasant food and resilient, lovely people.

Venice and Verona neatly symbolize the refinement of the Veneto, where technique and high standards mean that liver is exalted with all-star status, and rice cooked with peas (risi e bisi) becomes a signature dish. The polenta is white and creamy, the artichokes tiny and tender, the agrodolce dishes neither too sweet nor too sour. The fish market of Venice is a cook's dream, the nearby vegetable market a cornucopia. Napoleon called the city's Piazza San Marco "Europe's living room," and he may still be right. Verona's Piazza Bra can almost compete historically—Garibaldi roused the populace to Italian unity and glory from a balcony there, across the street from the ancient Roman coliseum, where gladiatorial combat has been replaced by opera.

These three regions are also still showing the sophistication that kept them a step or two ahead of the rest of Italy's wine areas for centuries. It's a large territory, producing vast amounts of wine. French varieties such as Cabernet Franc, Carmenere, Chardonnay, Sauvignon Blanc, and Merlot have been here for more than a hundred years, joined in the last few decades by Cabernet Sauvignon. Most of them were pretty bland, but being non-Italian, they gained some acceptance because they seemed exotic. Now, with the rest of the world also marketing these varieties, there's pressure to improve.

The new types of international-style wines are either more concentrated and oaky, or blended with a little bit of one or another of the native varieties. Most of the former aren't bad, some are very good, and a few might be great, just like the wines of France, the United States, Chile, and Australia after which they're styled. Most of the latter lack definition and are just moderately interesting, slightly offbeat wines.

There is still plenty of exciting wine left over, though. Some relatively light reds shine, especially valuable as international-style reds grow increasingly heavy, and the snappy whites are also a wonderful, refreshing relief from overbearing Chardonnays. In Friuli, a growing number of what are called Superwhites have appeared, blends of Pinot Bianco, Sauvignon Blanc, Tocai Friulano, sometimes a little Riesling, and maybe a bit of Chardonnay, the latter for a muscular boost. They may be called simply bianco (white), or carry fantasy names, like Vintage Tunina or Molmatta, but they're easy to identify by their price tags, which are hefty.

Sparkling Wine

Prosecco

This lightly sparkling, delightful wine is Venice's favorite sipping wine and an Italian original. Prosecco is an ancient grape of the Veneto that was in decline until the late nineteenth century, when the *Charmat* method of producing sparkling wine in bulk quantities arrived. Light and fresh, Prosecco was the perfect partner for bubbles, and got a new lease on life as a wine to be taken easily, the essence of refined hedonism.

Today, the increasingly sophisticated technology of the area, bolstered by the well-respected school and research center at Conegliano Veneto, has benefited the wine even more. Carefully controlled cold fermentation preserves the prized aromas and delicate fruitiness, while stainless-steel tanks keep the wine fresh and focused, crisp and lightly citric, with a faintly floral aroma.

For a long time, Prosecco was softly sweet and *frizzante,* "slightly sparkling." These days, many of the wines are slightly drier and *spumante,* "fully sparkling" (twice as much atmospheric pressure as *frizzante*), with a small percentage of Pinot Blanc or Pinot Grigio blended in. Wines labeled "brut" tend to be *amabile,* that is to say, soft and not the least austere, while those labeled "extra dry" tend to flirt their way just over the sweetness line; most winemakers believe that absolute, total dryness would eliminate Prosecco's character. In other words, a certain level of sugar, even if not perceptible as sweetness, is necessary to bring up the aroma. Versions labeled *"superiore"* really are superior, having a little more alcohol and finer flavor. In Venice, Prosecco is taken in small glasses at any time of the day—the drink of sociability. In more puritan circles, it's a lovely aperitif.

TYPICAL AROMAS AND FLAVORS

Hints of delicate white peaches and green apples, perhaps a touch of apricots, and an impression of almonds in the aftertaste.

TIPS TO SUCCESSFUL MATCHES
WITH PROSECCO

- *Low alcohol makes Prosecco a great sipping wine, and the hint of sweetness combined with crispness makes it a match for fish and shellfish antipasti, such as cold shrimp, crab cakes, fried squid, and smoked whitefish.*
- *Foods with a salty aspect, especially sliced ham, prosciutto with melon, scallops wrapped in bacon, and cheese toasts, fit in nicely.*

Red Wines

Valpolicella

Valpolicella is one of Italy's most underrated wines, victimized by its past a generation ago, when a flood of mass-produced, mediocre, and slightly sour wine arrived in America and went straight to pizza joints. As soon as most of us could afford to move up from this cheap stuff, we did, and never looked back. If we still aren't, we're missing something. Valpolicella is reinventing itself, and is more than a pleasant surprise. It's getting serious, without being ponderous.

It is a blend of grapes, most of them unique to the Veneto. Corvina is the main grape, aromatic and acidic, with a strong, juicy, red-cherry flavor, followed by Rondinella, also aromatic and contributing color as well, and any one of several others that act as seasoning or beef up the blend a little, including small amounts of Merlot and Cabernet Sauvignon. There was always a hierarchy of wines built up from this cornerstone, and in the last decade or so, several more layers have been added.

The basic wine, the standard version, is known as the *normale,* sometimes designated Classico, sometimes not. The Classico name tells you that the wine comes from the original zone up in the hills, and it's usually a little better than the non-Classico (though not always; taste some and see for yourself). It's intended as a cheap and cheery, moderately hearty, refreshing, quite unpretentious wine that is meant to be drunk soon after the vintage date without thinking much about it. One great advantage is that it's light bodied. In a world where so much wine is becoming heavy and ponderous, that's a quality to be esteemed.

Most of the categories above the *normale* depend on different ways of making the wine more intense, ratcheting up the flavor. The top level of intensity and flavor—and, certainly, price—is Amarone. It is made from the same mix of grapes, but the grapes are dried in lofts for several months, which concentrates their character and sugar levels, before being crushed and fermented into dense, inky, powerhouse wines. As one winemaker told me, "Making these wines is like squeezing marmalade." They have a *minimum* alcohol content of 14 percent by law, and are usually aged for several years before being sold. Amarones come in two styles, the popular bold and dry (very good with game, especially boar or venison), and the more rare moderately sweet (wonderful after dinner, especially with strong cheese).

There are several medium-bodied wines in between that are pleasant and delicious, but a little more weighty, sharing just a little of the same sort of intensity as Amarone, thanks to a process known as *ripasso,* "passed over again." Basically, *normale* wine is made in the autumn, and Amarone in the spring. *Ripasso* wines are made when a selection of *normale* is poured over the grape skins and pulp left over from making Amarone, which causes the *normale* wine to ferment again, mildly but enough to gain some extra character, color, and strength. Yet another variation pours the wine directly over dried grapes, with the same effect. Usually, somewhere on the front or back label, there will be a reference to *ripasso,* or a phrase like "the soul of the Veneto," but most often these wines come under the *superiore* category. Some splendid single-vineyard Valpolicellas are also *ripasso,* robust but elegant and usually twice the price of the standard version, but well worth it.

TYPICAL AROMAS AND FLAVORS OF VALPOLICELLA

Dried cherries predominate, backed by some of the juiciness of black cherries and raspberries; in the single-vineyard ripasso *category, there are usually added flavors, hints of blackberries, and a herbal note in the aftertaste.*

TYPICAL AROMAS AND FLAVORS OF AMARONE

All the above, but richer and more concentrated, plus blackberry jam, resin, cinnamon, and a very slight bittersweet bite in the aftertaste.

TIPS TO SUCCESSFUL MATCHES
WITH VALPOLICELLA AND AMARONE

- *The standard versions are good, easygoing, nearly all-purpose house wines for casual food or occasions. They are terrific with rich vegetable dishes such as pumpkin or spinach ravioli, or sausage risotto, stuffed eggplant, grilled chicken, ham, pork, or tuna salad.*
- *You can lightly chill the standard versions to gain a little refreshment value without sacrificing flavor, which adds to their versatility.*
- *Medium-weight* ripasso *or* superiore *versions are good enough, and savory enough, to be perfect partners for more elegant occasions and meals, especially with braised meat or roast pork or turkey.*
- *Most dry Amarone, though blockbuster wine, has enough finesse to pair well with full-flavored food, like rich osso buco or a thick charcoal-grilled rare steak, and can also carry you on past dinner, if you're finishing with strong cheeses.*

- *Italians consider the sweeter version of Amarone a* vino da meditazione *(literally, "meditation wine"), a wine worthy of such respect that it can stand alone as something to sip quietly after dinner. But they're also happy to do some thinking over a glass and a hunk of fine blue cheese, and perhaps a few fresh walnuts.*

Bardolino

Bardolino is basically a junior version of standard Valpolicella, even lighter and mostly simpler, with a slightly bitter aftertaste. It doesn't travel well, which means that unless you're near where it was made, you have to kiss a lot of frogs to get a princely one. In pursuit of commercial success, a couple of other styles have evolved, the most interesting a cherry pink, refreshing *rosato* called Chiaretto, worth drinking if it's no more than a year old and it's a hot day in northern Italy.

Refosco

Outside of the Veneto, the northeastern corner of Italy is fragmented in terms of wine: a lot of different varieties, odd juxtapositions of ancient and modern, historical and experimental, grapes and wines with unfamiliar names like Pignolo, Raboso, Lagrein, Teroldego, Schiava (meaning "female slave," surely not an image builder), Tazzeleghe ("tongue cutter," a good example of truth in labeling). Refosco is also somewhat unfamiliar, but is coming on, often considered to be a potential star of the region and in international markets. Although it has a medium-weight body, it looks and feels light, an impression reinforced by its considerably fragrant mixed-wildflower aroma. It's refreshingly tart, with a pleasantly bitter, dry aftertaste. Not a wine to drink casually, it needs food, preferably something moderately rich, like roast pork or spicy sausages, or strong cheeses, such as *Montasio*. Worth seeking out.

Schioppettino

Usually this wine is just a footnote in wine texts, but I'm assured by several winemakers in Friuli that it's on the rise and destined for stardom. I hope so. It's just plain nice, and very different. The color is deep purple, the aroma is of violets and cherries, and the flavor is reminiscent of black cherries, with a pleasant, slightly bitter and persistent aftertaste, a well-balanced package. It tends to be firm, but not overly tannic. There are basically two styles: light and meant to be enjoyed young, which is the standard, and a fuller, more tannic version, aged in small French oak barrels, slightly spicy, and meant to be aged further, even a decade after the vintage. The former would be fine with sausages or tuna, the latter with steak or venison. Both are worth seeking out.

Soave

Soave was once the most popular Italian wine in America, especially after Frank Sinatra said it was his favorite. Since then, we've discovered the wide variety Italy offers, and several other reds and whites have crowded into the top level. But the best Soaves are still among Italy's best white wines, and are particularly superb as partners for seafood.

Soave is a blended wine, traditionally a mix of mostly Garganega and a little Trebbiano di Soave, a simple recipe that yields a lovely, moderately light wine with a slightly flowery aroma and a lingering flavor reminiscent of very ripe, juicy apples or pears. Good Soave is always a pleasant surprise, because its initial impressions are so quiet that you expect them to fade away, but then its crisp flavor just keeps on rolling across your palate, polite but unstoppable.

The best Soaves are labeled "Classico," which means that the grapes come from a specific zone of vineyards up on the slopes of ancient volcanic hillsides to the west of Verona. Blessed by sunshine and cool breezes that allow them to reach their full potential, the flavors of the Garganega grape become quite expansive and pronounced, openly fruity and with a fine-tuned snap of acidity, while the Trebbiano di Soave's wildflower aromas blossom, making the blend a perfect partnership. About 25 percent of all Soave is Classico.

The remainder is from grapes grown on the plains down below the hills. The soil is richer and the climate is warmer because there isn't much of a breeze, so the wines tend to be less elegant, not as complex or persistently flavored. Down here, in order to boost the flavor and body of the wines, some Chardonnay or Pinot Bianco can be added to the blend, and the version of Trebbiano used is Trebbiano Toscano, a pretty ordinary but prolific grape. The reason for all this nontraditional tinkering and fiddling around is that Soave's great success inspired commercially minded winemakers to expand the zone, and the new vineyard areas weren't ideal. What it comes down to is that most of the wine labeled simply "Soave" is simply ordinary white wine. It may be cheap—it certainly should be—but it won't usually be very good value.

There is one other word on the label that can be misleading, *superiore*. It merely means that the wine contains slightly more alcohol than usual, because the grapes were a little more ripe at harvesttime. It doesn't make the wine any better, just stronger.

TYPICAL AROMAS AND FLAVORS
The lightly floral aroma is usually matched by a mix of light melon and peach flavors, with a bit of almond and a refreshing, stony mineral aspect in the aftertaste.

TIPS TO SUCCESSFUL MATCHES WITH SOAVE
- *Soave marries best with aromatic and somewhat complex fish dishes, as its mix of aromas heighten those of the food, while its persistent acidity shores up the flavors.*
- *Moderately flavored herbs and spices, and combinations of them, work best, complementing, rather than contrasting, with the wine.*
- *To make the most of its medium fullness, serve Soave with first courses, including seafood salads, or rich pasta dishes, rather than as a sipping wine or with appetizers.*

Lugana and Bianco di Custoza

These are two blended wines from two different regions, Lombardy and the Veneto, but from vineyards south of Lake Garda that aren't far apart. The grape blends are similar, not only to each other but also to Soave. The wines are generally lighter than Soave, in flavor and aroma, making them best as a simple drink, with the added attraction that they're usually reasonably priced and thus good value.

Pinot Grigio

Pinot Grigio is the fastest-growing wine in America in almost every way: imports from Italy are soaring ahead of the pack, and vineyards devoted to the grape are expanding rapidly in California and Oregon (it's also newly popular in New Zealand and Argentina, so it's probably not a short-term fad). In Italy, the typical color of the wine is a pretty shade of onionskin, showing a slight coppery tinge. Even the best of the wines, from the hills and high plains of Friuli, aren't necessarily complex, but they have lovely, lasting flavors reminiscent of peach and apricot. Versions from the flatter, lower-lying areas tend to be a little diffuse, but have at least a pronounced apple character. Pinot Grigio is not a high-acid wine, but there's a clean, fresh, almost rocky mineral quality to the aftertaste that makes it refreshing. There is a small tendency lately to age the wine for a short time in oak, which mellows it out, but in my opinion doesn't improve its character. If you taste a Pinot Grigio that seems plump and round, rather than crisp, it is probably one of these.

TYPICAL AROMAS AND FLAVORS
Apricots, peaches, sometimes apples, slight hint of citrus and herbs in the aftertaste.

TIPS TO SUCCESSFUL MATCHES WITH PINOT GRIGIO
- *Its persistent but moderate flavor makes Pinot Grigio a good partner for moderately voluptuous pasta dishes, such as penne in a cream or cheese sauce, or spaghetti tossed with butter and sage and grated Parmesan, as well as gnocchi with various rich sauces.*
- *The mineral edge on its aftertaste makes a good fit with freshwater fish, such as trout, perch, or catfish, and some small flatfish, such as plaice, sand dabs, or rockfish, especially when crisply sautéed with herbs.*

Pinot Bianco

A cousin of Pinot Grigio, Pinot Bianco usually doesn't get nearly the respect it deserves, except from the locals in Friuli, and especially the winemakers themselves—it's their preferred white wine, I'm told. It's valued as much for its creamy texture, something of a middle-weight plumpness, as for its teasing mix of aromas and flavors (not easily pinned down but fresh and lively) and its crisp aftertaste. Most Pinot Bianco in northern Italy goes into pretty good Champagne-style sparkling wine, which is fair enough. In Friuli, especially in the same high, cool Collio and Colli Orientali del Friuli areas where Pinot Grigio flourishes, it makes a modestly distinguished wine worth seeking out.

TYPICAL AROMAS AND FLAVORS
A tight mix of green apples, melons, and wildflowers, with a hint of vanilla, and almonds in the aftertaste.

TIPS TO SUCCESSFUL MATCHES WITH PINOT BIANCO
- *Follow through on the suggestion of almonds in the aftertaste by pairing Pinot Bianco with earthy flavors, such as white fish sautéed or roasted with mushrooms or trout in a sauce with slivered almonds.*
- *Pinot Bianco has enough acidity and complexity to match elegant preparations of cold meats, such as* bresaola, *carpaccio of beef, or* prosciutto di San Daniele.

Sauvignon Blanc

This is another French grape that has gone native in Italy, most notably in Friuli, where its sometimes shrill acidity is modulated into fresh and citrus crispness, and the rudely acidic aspect of its character so often found in France and New Zealand disappears. What's left is the best of what the grape has to offer: lightly grassy aroma (think of a freshly cut lawn) mingled with faint hints of grapefruit and orange and a suggestion of flowers, with a vibrant acidity that wakes up your palate and sets you up for more. Sauvignon Blanc is undoubtedly one of Italy's best white wines, especially from Collio, Colli Orientali del Friuli, or Alto Adige.

TYPICAL AROMAS AND FLAVORS
Green grass, grapefruit, oranges, and sometimes hints of peaches and fresh red peppers and herbs.

TIPS TO SUCCESSFUL MATCHES
WITH SAUVIGNON BLANC

- *Try to match Sauvignon Blanc's complexity and elegance, especially aiming for the same sort of resin-herbal notes: sea bass baked with white wine and tarragon, halibut with tarragon-mustard sauce, turbot fillets grilled with rosemary, or rockfish fillets sautéed with dill.*
- *Sauvignon Blanc and garlic are a match made in gastronomic heaven: a fireworks show for your palate, the* 1812 Overture *with real cannons, your first good kiss, one of the nicest "wow factors" you'll encounter in the world of wine.*

Tocai Friulano

This is the native grape of Friuli, producing an austere wine, very dry and aloof when it's young, needing several years to mellow into some sort of pleasant companion. Even then, it will never be amiable, let alone the life of the party, but it will be unique and fascinating, with hints of exotic spice aromas mingling with firm fruit flavors, and a distinctly dry, mineral aftertaste that always reminds me of the pebbles my friends and I used to slip under our tongues to keep from getting thirsty on long hikes. It's fairly rare, and usually somewhat expensive, the sort of wine to try if someone else is buying. The best versions come from the Collio zone, where the climate teases more flavor from the grapes.

TYPICAL AROMAS AND FLAVORS
Moderate amounts of tangerine, dried apricot, vague hints of cinnamon and clove, and mineral aftertaste.

TIP TO SUCCESSFUL MATCHES
WITH TOCAI FRIULANO

- *The austerity of Tocai Friulano can be turned into a virtue when it's paired with strongly flavored seafood, such as bluefish or mackerel, or with highly spiced Thai or Sichuan dishes.*

Northeast **:**
Recipes

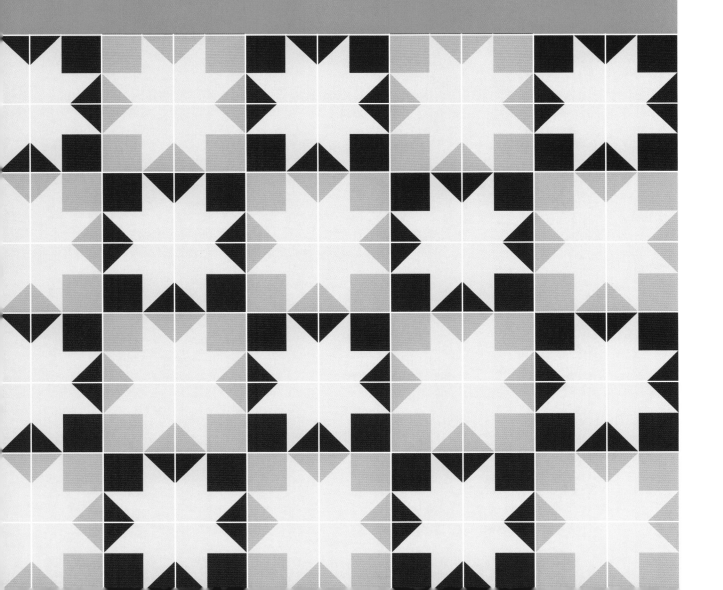

Pear Salad with Walnuts and Cheese

RECOMMENDED WINE: **Pinot Grigio**
ALTERNATIVE WINE: **Asti Spumante**

Vinegar is generally an enemy of wine, throwing the flavor off, but balsamic vinegar, which is aged and mellowed in wood barrels, is gentle enough to fit well, acting more as a flavoring agent than anything else. The *grana padano* cheese, from the Veneto, is grainy and flaky and similar to *Parmigiano-Reggiano,* but less expensive; either works equally well here, but anything labeled "Parmesan" isn't anywhere near being an acceptable substitute. This salad, meant to be served at room temperature, could work equally well as a first course or to finish a dinner, instead of dessert (my wife and I often serve it that way in the summer, after a light meal). The best choice at the beginning of a meal would be a fresh and fruity still wine, while the latter choice would get a good lift from slight sweetness and bubbles.

20 to 24 golden raisins

20 walnut halves

1 tablespoon balsamic vinegar

3 tablespoons extra-virgin olive oil

salt and freshly ground black pepper

2 pears such as Anjou, Bosc, or Bartlett

8 ounces *grana padano* cheese, shaved into flakes

SERVES 4

IN A SMALL BOWL, soak the raisins in warm water to cover for 30 minutes to soften. Drain and pat dry with paper towels.

PREHEAT THE OVEN TO 350°F. Spread the walnut halves on a baking sheet and toast in the oven for 6 or 7 minutes. Remove from the oven and transfer to a bowl to cool.

IN A SMALL BOWL, whisk together the vinegar and olive oil, and then whisk in a little salt and pepper to taste to create a vinaigrette. Set aside.

PEEL, HALVE, AND CORE THE PEARS, then cut each half lengthwise into thin slices, keeping the slices together. Place a sliced pear half on each plate and, holding the blossom end together, spread the slices, creating a fan effect. Scatter the raisins and walnuts evenly over the pears. Drizzle with the vinaigrette. Scatter the cheese on top and serve at once.

Pennine with Flaked Fish Fillets and Olive Marmalade

RECOMMENDED WINE: **Pinot Bianco**
ALTERNATIVE WINE: **Pinot Grigio**

The lightness of most flaky fish calls for a similar lightness in the wine, and for this recipe, a wonderful first course from my favorite restaurant in Venice, Osteria alle Testiere, the Veneto offers a multitude of perfect partners that can help out without showing off. The keynote is crisp dryness that supports the complex but subtle hints of olive, tomato, and basil surrounding the fish and pasta, and lightness appropriate to opening a meal.

6 ounces *pennine* or other small tubular pasta

extra-virgin olive oil for tossing pasta,
   plus 2 tablespoons

1 teaspoon minced garlic

2 tablespoons Olive Marmalade (page 200)

1 tablespoon tomato purée

4 fresh basil leaves, torn into small pieces

¾ cup dry white wine

¾ cup fish stock or bottled clam juice

salt and freshly ground black pepper

4 white fish fillets such as rockfish, snapper,
   sand dabs, or rex sole, 6 to 8 ounces each, skinned

1 tablespoon chopped fresh parsley

SERVES 4 AS A FIRST COURSE

BRING A LARGE POT FILLED WITH SALTED WATER TO A BOIL. Add the pasta, stir well, and cook until almost done, about 6 minutes. Drain the pasta, rinse with cold water, and toss with a little olive oil to keep it from sticking together. Set aside.

IN A WIDE HEAVY-BOTTOMED SAUCEPAN, combine the 2 tablespoons olive oil, garlic, Olive Marmalade, tomato purée, basil, wine, and stock. Season with salt and pepper. Stir well and bring to a simmer over low heat. Place the fish in the pan, cover, and cook until the fish is opaque throughout and just firm, about 6 minutes. Remove the cover and flake the fish in the pan, using a pair of forks to pull the fillets apart gently against the grain into coarse shreds.

ADD THE PASTA AND THE PARSLEY TO THE FISH MIXTURE AND STIR GENTLY TO MIX THOROUGHLY. Raise the heat to medium and cook for about 2 minutes, to heat through, stirring once or twice.

DIVIDE THE PASTA AND FISH AMONG WARMED SHALLOW BOWLS, including just enough of the liquid to moisten thoroughly. Serve at once.

Spaghetti in *Bresaola-Rosemary Sauce*

RECOMMENDED WINE: **Soave**
ALTERNATIVE WINE: **Valpolicella**

Lake Garda, in the north of Italy, is nearly alpine, but it acts as a kind of thermostat, and the climate is surprisingly mild. The lake is actually north of the line where olives can supposedly grow, but there they are, and delicately delicious, too. Much of the food is marked by an elegant lightness, as in this pasta dish, which features *bresaola,* air-dried, aged beef fillet that is thinly sliced. The wine needs to be light as well, and either red or white works, as long as it's fruity and crisp.

> 1 tablespoon golden raisins
>
> 2 tablespoons chopped fresh rosemary
>
> 1 teaspoon kosher salt
>
> 4 tablespoons extra-virgin olive oil,
>   plus extra for serving
>
> 12 ounces spaghetti
>
> 4 ounces *bresaola,* cut into ½-inch dice
>
> ½ cup walnuts, chopped
>
> freshly ground black pepper

SERVES 4 AS A FIRST COURSE

IN A SMALL BOWL, soak the raisins in warm water to cover for 30 minutes to soften. Drain, pat dry with paper towels, and chop roughly. In a mortar, combine the raisins, rosemary, salt, and 1 tablespoon of the olive oil, and grind with a pestle to make a rough paste. (Alternatively, mix together in a small bowl with the back of a spoon.)

BRING A LARGE POT FILLED WITH SALTED WATER TO A BOIL. Add the pasta, stir well, and cook until al dente, about 11 minutes.

WHILE THE PASTA IS COOKING, heat the remaining 3 tablespoons olive oil over medium heat in a heavy-bottomed saucepan or skillet large enough to accommodate the pasta later. Add the *bresaola,* rosemary mixture, and walnuts, stir well, and cook until the *bresaola* begins to change color, 2 to 3 minutes. Drain the pasta, add to the pan, and season with pepper. Stir well to coat the pasta thoroughly with the sauce.

DIVIDE THE PASTA EVENLY AMONG WARMED SHALLOW BOWLS. Drizzle a little olive oil over each portion and serve at once.

Duck *Ragù* and Tagliatelle on Pea Sauce with Pecorino

RECOMMENDED WINE: **Soave Classico Superiore**
ALTERNATIVE WINE: **Pinot Grigio**

Verona is, of course, the setting for *Romeo and Juliet,* as well as home to an impressive coliseum, nearly as awesome as Rome's. It's also a prosperous and sophisticated city. On its outskirts is the palatial Hotel Villa del Quar, a luxurious converted Renaissance villa with a superb kitchen and wine cellar. Chef Bruno Barbieri is very intense and very focused, and so is this creation of his. Even though duck is red meat, the long cooking mellows it, and the richness of the dish calls for something light and crisp that won't fight it, yet has enough flavor to strike a balance.

DUCK *RAGÙ:*

½ cup olive oil

½ cup minced celery

½ cup minced carrot

½ cup minced onion

12 ounces duck meat (from about 2 breast halves), skinned and roughly chopped

¼ cup tomato paste

bouquet garni: 2 fresh thyme sprigs, 2 fresh parsley sprigs, and 1 bay leaf, tied together with kitchen string

PEA SAUCE:

1 cup reduced-sodium canned chicken broth

1 tablespoon olive oil

3 ounces prosciutto, chopped

3 ounces pancetta, chopped

1 onion, chopped

1 clove garlic, chopped

8 ounces thawed frozen petite peas

1 teaspoon chopped fresh rosemary

1 teaspoon chopped fresh sage

1 pound dried tagliatelle

FOR SERVING:

4 tablespoons extra-virgin olive oil

aged pecorino cheese, shaved into flakes

SERVES 4 AS A MAIN COURSE

TO MAKE THE *RAGÙ*, in a heavy-bottomed saucepan, heat the olive oil over low heat. Add the celery, carrot, and onion and cook, stirring occasionally, until they begin to soften and give off moisture, about 10 minutes. Add the duck meat and stir well to blend. Continue to cook, stirring occasionally, until the moisture is almost gone, 6 or 7 minutes. Add the tomato paste, bouquet garni, and enough water to cover the mixture. Cover, reduce the heat to the lowest setting, and simmer for about 1½ hours, checking every now and then to make sure it doesn't dry out and adding a little water if necessary. When the sauce is ready, the duck should be meltingly tender. Discard the bouquet garni.

WHILE THE *RAGÙ* IS COOKING, make the pea sauce: In a small saucepan, bring the broth to a simmer. Meanwhile, in a heavy-bottomed saucepan, heat the olive oil over medium heat. Add the prosciutto, pancetta, onion, and garlic and cook, stirring, until the prosciutto and pancetta begin to brown, 3 to 4 minutes. Add the peas, rosemary, and sage, stir well, and cook for 2 minutes more. Add the broth and cook until the peas are tender, about 3 minutes longer. Remove from the heat. In a food processor or blender, purée the mixture until smooth. Set aside. (This sauce can be made up to 3 hours in advance, cooled, and refrigerated until needed, then gently reheated.)

BRING A LARGE POT FILLED WITH SALTED WATER TO A BOIL. Add the pasta, stir well, and cook until al dente, about 11 minutes. Drain.

TO SERVE, gently reheat the *ragù* and the pea sauce. Pour a thin layer of the pea sauce onto each warmed plate or shallow bowl. Divide the pasta evenly among the plates, placing it on top of the pea sauce. Spoon the *ragù* over the pasta, again dividing evenly. Drizzle each portion with 1 tablespoon of the olive oil and sprinkle with flakes of pecorino cheese.

NOTE: *Chef Barbieri garnishes this dish with a* cresta di gallo, *or "rooster's comb," which he simmers with carrot, celery, and onion for three hours and then cuts into small cubes. I think it's a case of gilding the lily, but if you wish to try it, poultry shops in your local Chinatown or kosher poultry butchers are usually the best sources.*

Soused Pasta with
Tangy Cheese Sauce

RECOMMENDED WINE: **Refosco**
ALTERNATIVE WINE: **Valpolicella**

The idea of cooking pasta in wine is fairly widespread around Italy's vineyards. Adolfo Folonari of Ruffino cooks his pasta in Chianti, but then he has a ready supply down in his cellar. In Liguria, it's known as *pasta alla deficeira,* rude slang for someone who's not very bright, and in the Veneto the pasta is *ubriachi,* for "drunken" (even though most of the alcohol evaporates during cooking). Wine gives it an unusual flavor that is accentuated by the cheese. *Montasio* is a cow's milk cheese (see page 211). It's rich and tangy, but Asiago is an acceptable substitute. Two bottles of wine may seem lavish, but an inexpensive light red, such as Valpolicella or Refosco, is perfectly fine, and, if stored properly after the pasta is drained (in a tightly capped jar in the refrigerator for up to 3 days), it can be reused to flavor a wine sauce or risotto.

1 tablespoon olive oil

1 celery stalk, cut into ½-inch chunks

2 carrots, peeled and cut into ½-inch chunks

2 shallots, chopped

salt and freshly ground black pepper

2 bottles (750 ml each) dry red wine

12 ounces penne or other short tubular pasta

6 tablespoons unsalted butter

8 ounces *Montasio* cheese, grated

2 tablespoons chopped fresh parsley

good pinch of freshly grated nutmeg

6 fresh basil leaves, torn in half

SERVES 4 AS A HEARTY MAIN COURSE

IN A LARGE HEAVY-BOTTOMED SAUCEPAN, heat the olive oil over medium-low heat. Add the celery, carrots, and shallots and cook, stirring occasionally, until softened, about 5 minutes. Season with salt and pepper. Add the wine, raise the heat to medium, and let the sauce simmer for 10 minutes. Turn up the heat and bring the liquid to a boil. Add the pasta, stir well, and cook until al dente, about 11 minutes.

JUST BEFORE THE PASTA IS READY, in another large saucepan, melt the butter over medium-low heat. Drain the pasta and vegetables (quickly, not fully; they should have liquid clinging to them), reserving the liquid for another use. Off the heat, put the pasta and vegetables in the saucepan with the butter and stir well. Return to medium-low heat and add the cheese, parsley, and nutmeg. Shake the pan and stir the pasta gently but thoroughly to distribute and melt the cheese.

DIVIDE THE PASTA AMONG WARMED SHALLOW BOWLS. Garnish each portion with the basil and serve at once.

Butternut Squash Risotto with Prosciutto

RECOMMENDED WINE: **Pinot Grigio**
ALTERNATIVE WINE: **Sauvignon Blanc**

Italians took to pumpkins just as they did to such other New World foods as tomatoes and corn. In the autumn, pumpkin appears on menus as stuffing for ravioli, as a flavoring in cookies, and in risotto. My favorite when the weather turns cold is another member of the family, butternut squash, which has more flavor and doesn't fall apart as easily. Spiked with a touch of rosemary and boosted by the savory taste of prosciutto, this risotto is a sophisticated, simple lunch.

7 cups reduced-sodium canned chicken broth

1 tablespoon unsalted butter

2 tablespoons olive oil

1 onion, finely chopped

1 clove garlic, finely chopped

2 cups Arborio rice

1 large fresh rosemary sprig

1 cup dry white wine

2 cups cubed, peeled butternut squash
  ($\frac{1}{2}$-inch cubes)

$\frac{1}{2}$ cup chopped prosciutto

1 tablespoon chopped fresh parsley

SERVES 4 AS A MAIN COURSE

POUR THE BROTH INTO A SAUCEPAN AND BRING TO A SIMMER ON A BACK BURNER. Adjust the heat to maintain a bare simmer. In a heavy-bottomed saucepan, melt the butter with the olive oil over low heat. Add the onion and garlic and cook, stirring occasionally, until soft, about 5 minutes. Increase the heat to medium and add the rice and rosemary to the pan. Stir vigorously to coat all the grains with the fat, and cook, stirring, until opaque, 2 to 3 minutes. Add the wine and cook, stirring, until nearly absorbed. Add half the squash and $\frac{1}{2}$ cup of the broth and cook, stirring frequently, until the broth is absorbed. Add the remainder of the squash to the simmering broth. (This is so it will cook, but keep its shape; the squash in the rice will probably break down into fragments, which is fine.) Continue adding the broth, $\frac{1}{2}$ cup at a time and waiting until it is absorbed before adding more. Stir gently and often.

AFTER 15 MINUTES, stir in the prosciutto. Then, using a slotted spoon, scoop out the remainder of the squash from the broth and add it to the rice. Stir gently to distribute evenly. Return to adding the broth. After another 5 minutes, test the rice for doneness. The rice is ready when the grains are tender but slightly firm in the center. If it is not ready, cook for another 2 minutes or so. If it is still firm and you have no more stock, add $\frac{1}{2}$ cup hot water and cook until absorbed.

REMOVE THE ROSEMARY SPRIG AND DISCARD. Divide the risotto evenly among warmed shallow bowls and garnish with the parsley. Serve at once.

Seafood Risotto, *Venetian Style*

RECOMMENDED WINE: **Pinot Bianco**
ALTERNATIVE WINE: **Sauvignon Blanc**

They do things differently in Venice: their favorite dried cod is air-dried and not salted, unlike the rest of Italy's classic *baccalà*, and they have elevated liver and onions to an elegant signature dish. One of the most intriguing variations is the local seafood risotto, which is creamy, light, and refined, and uses the best of the incredible variety of fish in the lagoon to create flavors that are persistent and complex. The wine should be the best sort of crisp, even austere white, such as the stars of Friuli, from the fabled Collio or Colli Orientali areas.

STOCK:

8 ounces shrimp

3 celery stalks, coarsely chopped

2 onions, coarsely chopped

2 carrots, peeled and coarsely chopped

1 fennel bulb, coarsely chopped, or
    2 tablespoons fennel seeds

1 bunch fresh parsley, coarsely chopped

4 fresh thyme sprigs

2 bay leaves

1 lemon, cut in half

8 black peppercorns

2 quarts water

1 cup bottled clam juice

2 tablespoons olive oil

1 small onion, finely chopped

2 cups Arborio rice

1 cup dry white wine

8 ounces rockfish, cod, or other flaky
    white fish fillets, skinned and finely chopped

6 ounces salmon fillet, skinned and
    cut into 1-inch chunks

2 tablespoons finely chopped fresh parsley

SERVES 6 AS A FIRST COURSE

TO MAKE THE STOCK, peel and devein the shrimp, reserving the shells. Put the shrimp in a bowl of cold water to cover, and refrigerate. In a saucepan, combine all the vegetables, parsley, thyme, bay leaves, lemon, and peppercorns. Pour in the water and bring to a boil. Reduce the heat to a gentle simmer, add the shells, and cook, partially covered, for 1 hour. Remove from the heat, strain through a fine-mesh sieve, and discard the solids. Return the stock to the pan, add the clam juice, and bring to a simmer on a back burner. Adjust the heat to maintain a bare simmer.

IN A HEAVY-BOTTOMED SAUCEPAN, heat the olive oil over low heat. Add the onion and cook, stirring occasionally, until soft, about 5 minutes. Increase the heat to medium and add the rice to the pan. Stir vigorously to coat all the grains with the oil and cook, stirring, until opaque, 2 to 3 minutes. Add the wine and cook, stirring constantly, until nearly absorbed. Add about $\frac{1}{2}$ cup of the stock and cook, stirring frequently, until absorbed. Continue adding the stock, $\frac{1}{2}$ cup at a time and waiting until it is absorbed before adding more. Stir gently and often to keep the rice from sticking.

DRAIN THE SHRIMP AND FINELY CHOP THEM. When the rice has been cooking for about 10 minutes, add the shrimp and rock-fish to it. At the same time, place the salmon chunks in a small, heavy-bottomed saucepan, ladle about 1 cup of the stock over them, place over medium heat, and poach for 3 to 4 minutes. Remove from the heat.

AFTER A TOTAL OF ABOUT 20 MINUTES, test the rice for doneness. It is ready when the grains are tender but slightly firm in the center and the mixture is creamy. If it is not ready, cook for another 2 minutes or so. If it is still firm and you have no more stock, add $\frac{1}{2}$ cup hot water and cook until absorbed.

DIVIDE THE RISOTTO EVENLY AMONG WARMED SHALLOW BOWLS. Using a slotted spoon, remove the salmon from the stock and arrange an equal amount on top of each portion. Sprinkle with the parsley and serve at once.

Baked Red Peppers Stuffed with Spinach, Shallots, and Sage

RECOMMENDED WINE: **Soave Classico**
ALTERNATIVE WINE: **Sauvignon Blanc**

This is a good accompaniment to grilled fish or chicken. It has enough kick to boost simple fare, and it looks good enough to complete a plate in style. It's as good eaten tepid as it is hot, so it's also a good choice to serve as part of a buffet.

3 tablespoons olive oil

2 pounds spinach, well rinsed and
tough stems removed

2 large red bell peppers, halved lengthwise,
seeded, and deribbed

4 shallots, finely chopped

2 tablespoons chopped fresh sage

6 tablespoons grated pecorino cheese

1 ½ teaspoons freshly ground black pepper

1 ½ cups water

SERVES 4

PREHEAT THE OVEN TO 350°F.

IN A LARGE SKILLET, heat 1 tablespoon of the olive oil over medium heat. Add the spinach, with just the rinsing water clinging to the leaves, cover, and cook just until wilted, about 2 minutes. Remove from the heat, drain in a sieve, rinse under cold water to cool, and press out any excess water. Chop finely and set aside.

PLACE THE BELL PEPPER HALVES ON A STEAMER RACK OVER RAPIDLY SIMMERING WATER, cover, and steam for 8 minutes to soften (or microwave on full power for the same amount of time). Transfer the pepper halves to a plate and set aside.

IN A LARGE SKILLET, heat the remaining 2 tablespoons olive oil over medium heat. Add the shallots and sauté until soft, about 5 minutes. Add the sage, stir well, and cook for 1 minute more. Remove from the heat.

IN A LARGE BOWL, combine the spinach, shallot-sage mixture, including any oil remaining in the skillet, 4 tablespoons of the cheese, and the black pepper. Mix well. Spoon the spinach mixture into the pepper halves, dividing it evenly, and sprinkle the tops with the remaining 2 tablespoons cheese.

PLACE THE PEPPER HALVES IN A BAKING DISH IN WHICH THEY FIT CLOSE TOGETHER, but not touching, and pour the water into the bottom of the dish. Bake the peppers until the filling is heated through and the peppers are tender, about 25 minutes. Serve hot, warm, or room temperature.

Fish Fillets in Aromatic Citrus Sauce

RECOMMENDED WINE: **Soave Classico**
ALTERNATIVE WINE: **Pinot Grigio**

Citrus flavors can be a little domineering, so they need to be balanced. Here, in a recipe from Osteria alle Testiere, one of Venice's most popular restaurants, an abundance of herbal notes keep them in check, while adding a bit of excitement of their own. You don't have to use every herb and spice listed—a majority of them will do—but don't skip the mint or star anise, which are the defining ones. Accompany the fish with a fairly sweet green vegetable, such as English peas or sugar snap peas, lightly tossed in butter. Pour a wine with full fruitiness and crispness, to balance the flavors.

2 tablespoons extra-virgin olive oil

½ teaspoon minced garlic

¾ cup fish stock or bottled clam juice

¼ cup fresh orange juice

¼ cup fresh lemon juice

1 tablespoon aromatics: good pinch each of
  chopped fresh mint, thyme, chives, tarragon,
  oregano, rosemary, basil, and sage; fennel seeds;
  ground coriander and cardamom; and 1 whole
  star anise

4 white fish fillets such as snapper, rockfish,
  or rex sole, skinned

4 cups hot steamed white rice

SERVES 4

IN A WIDE HEAVY-BOTTOMED SAUCEPAN, combine the olive oil, garlic, stock, orange and lemon juices, and the aromatics. Stir well and bring to a gentle simmer over low heat. Carefully place the fish fillets in the pan, cover, and poach until opaque throughout and just firm to the touch, about 6 minutes.

USING A SLOTTED SPATULA, remove the fish from the pan and place on a warmed heatproof plate in a warm oven. Bring the poaching liquid to a boil and boil for 3 minutes to reduce slightly, making a simple sauce.

PLACE AN EQUAL AMOUNT OF RICE ON EACH WARMED PLATE, top with a fish fillet, and spoon some sauce over each. Serve at once.

Turbot Braised in Valpolicella

RECOMMENDED WINE: **Valpolicella Classico**
ALTERNATIVE WINE: **Schioppettino**

In Italian, turbot is known as *rombo,* and the type found in the Mediterranean is generally smaller than the Atlantic variety. If you can find a small turbot, or a brill, which is a cousin, it is worth cooking the fish whole. The cooking time for a 2- to 3-pound fish is only slightly longer than for fillets, about 18 minutes. Leave the skin on until it's time to serve, and then scrape it off and lift the fillets right off the bone with a spatula. Pier Francesco Bolla, head of one of Verona's leading winemaking families, gave me this recipe in which the fish is cooked in Valpolicella. Have another bottle of light red handy to drink with it.

1 large onion, sliced into thin rings

4 turbot fillets, 6 to 8 ounces each, skinned

2 tablespoons all-purpose flour

2 tablespoons olive oil

1 clove garlic, peeled but left whole

1 large fresh thyme sprig

1 celery stalk, chopped

2 carrots, peeled and chopped

1 tablespoon juniper berries

1 cup coarsely chopped, peeled tomatoes

2 olive oil–packed anchovy fillets, chopped

1 1/2 cups Valpolicella

1 pound dried tagliatelle

1 tablespoon unsalted butter

4 ounces fresh white mushrooms, sliced

2 tablespoons finely chopped fresh parsley

SERVES 4

PREHEAT THE OVEN TO 350°F.

PLACE THE ONION SLICES IN A LAYER ON THE BOTTOM OF A ROASTING PAN. Dust the fish fillets lightly with the flour, shaking off the excess. In a large skillet, heat the olive oil with the garlic over medium heat. Working in batches if necessary, add the fish fillets and cook, turning once, until lightly golden, about 1 minute on each side. Remove the skillet from the heat and transfer the fish fillets to the roasting pan, placing them on top of the onion. Add the thyme, celery, carrots, juniper berries, tomatoes, anchovies, and wine to the skillet, return it to medium heat, and bring to a boil, scraping the pan bottom with a wooden spoon to loosen any browned bits. Reduce the heat to a strong simmer and reduce the liquid by about one-third, about 5 minutes.

POUR THE MIXTURE AROUND THE FISH, cover the roasting pan, and place in the oven to braise until the fish is opaque throughout and firm to a fingertip touch, about 15 minutes.

MEANWHILE, bring a large pot filled with salted water to a boil. Add the pasta, stir well, and cook until al dente, about 11 minutes. While the pasta is cooking, in a skillet, melt the butter over medium-high heat. Add the mushrooms and sauté until they brown and release their liquid, about 5 minutes.

WHEN THE PASTA IS READY, drain it, place in a warmed bowl, add the butter and mushrooms, and toss well. Divide the pasta among warmed shallow bowls. Using a spatula, carefully place a fish fillet on top of each serving of pasta. Pass the vegetable mixture in the roasting pan through a coarse-mesh sieve placed over a bowl, pressing it in with the back of a spoon. Spoon a few tablespoons of the pureé over each fish fillet. Garnish with the parsley and serve at once.

Sea Bass Roasted
in Red Wine Sauce

RECOMMENDED WINE: **Valpolicella Classico Superiore**
ALTERNATIVE WINE: **Refosco**

There is a splendid restaurant–wine bar in Verona called Antica Bottega del Vino (the Old Wine Shop). It is indeed very old, a cavernous room decorated with large wall frescoes, and it's always bustling, with waiters darting back and forth and a solid crowd at the small bar at the front. The wine list is encyclopedic. The food is not fancy, but it is superb. What takes most Americans aback is that this temple of gastronomy is usually swathed in a dense fog of cigarette smoke—it's the Italian way—and the mostly male crowd all seem to talk at the same time. I usually go to dinner here early, before the crowd arrives, and it's quieter and more breathable. One dish that's often on the menu is *branzino* in red wine, deliciously irresistible. Vegetables such as boiled potatoes and steamed green beans soak up the delicious sauce nicely.

> 5 tablespoons olive oil
>
> 6 shallots, chopped
>
> 2 cloves garlic, chopped
>
> 1 bay leaf
>
> 1 tablespoon chopped fresh marjoram
>
> 1 fresh rosemary sprig
>
> 2 cups dry red wine
>
> 2 tablespoons balsamic vinegar
>
> 2 sea bass, about 2 pounds each, cleaned
>
> salt and freshly ground black pepper
>
> 1 onion, sliced into thin rings
>
> 2 celery stalks, cut into 1/2-inch chunks
>
> 3 tomatoes, peeled, seeded, and chopped

SERVES 4

IN A HEAVY-BOTTOMED SAUCEPAN, heat 2 tablespoons of the olive oil over medium heat. Add the shallots and cook until soft, about 5 minutes. Add the garlic, bay leaf, marjoram, rosemary, and wine and bring to a boil. Boil rapidly until the liquid is reduced by half, about 10 minutes. Remove from the heat and strain through a fine-mesh sieve into a small bowl. Discard the solids. Add the balsamic vinegar and stir to mix. Set aside.

PREHEAT THE OVEN TO 400°F.

RINSE THE FISH AND DRY WELL. Using a sharp knife, score the skin with 3 diagonal slashes on each side. Rub the fish with 1 tablespoon of the olive oil and sprinkle with salt and pepper. Oil the bottom of a roasting pan with the remaining olive oil and place on the stove top over medium heat. Place the onion, celery, and tomatoes in the pan and heat through, shaking the pan frequently, until the vegetables release a little liquid, 3 or 4 minutes. Remove from the heat and place the fish on top of the vegetables in the pan. Pour the wine sauce evenly over the fish.

PUT THE PAN IN THE OVEN AND ROAST THE FISH, basting once halfway through, until the skin is lightly browned and the flesh is firm to the touch, about 25 minutes. Remove the pan from the oven, lift 1 fish from the pan, and place it on a work surface. To fillet it, make sideways cuts behind the head and before the tail, and then cut along the backbone from the head to the tail of the fish. Place the knife in that cut, parallel to the backbone, and work the knife down along the rib bones of the fish, from top to bottom. Lift off the fillet and place, skin side up, on a warmed plate. Turn the fish over and repeat the process, placing the second fillet on another warmed plate. Repeat with the remaining fish. Spoon the pan juices, including the onion, celery, and tomatoes, over the fillets and serve.

NOTE: *Because of overfishing, sea bass are getting smaller, so a 2-pound fish is average. A 3-pounder, if available, will also serve 4 people nicely. This recipe also works well for snapper or other types of bass.*

Chicken Thighs Stuffed with *Gremolata* in Prosciutto Parcels

RECOMMENDED WINE: **Sauvignon Blanc**

ALTERNATIVE WINE: **Tocai Friulano**

Gremolata is a vividly aromatic, sharp flavoring of parsley, lemon, and garlic meant to offset the richness of dishes like osso buco or lamb shanks. I also like to use a little on pan-roasted or braised fish, to add a zesty bite to the sauce, and have discovered that it goes well with the dark meat of chicken, especially when it's combined with the light saltiness of the prosciutto in these parcels. The final sauce is tartly flavorful, and matches especially well with green vegetables, such as asparagus, broccoli, or green beans. Mashed potatoes or polenta insure that no sauce is wasted.

> 2 tablespoons chopped fresh parsley
>
> 2 tablespoons grated lemon zest
>
> 2 cloves garlic, chopped
>
> 8 slices prosciutto
>
> 8 boneless, skinless chicken thighs
>
> salt and freshly ground black pepper
>
> 1/4 cup olive oil
>
> 1/4 cup dry white wine
>
> 2 tablespoons fresh lemon juice

SERVES 4

PREHEAT THE OVEN TO 325°F.

IN A SMALL BOWL, mix together the parsley, lemon zest, and garlic. Lay out the prosciutto slices on a work surface and place 1 chicken thigh, cut side up, on each slice. Season the thighs with salt and pepper. Spread each thigh with 1/8 of the parsley mixture, pressing it into the meat. Wrap the prosciutto around the thighs to enclose completely, forming parcels, and secure with toothpicks or tie with string.

IN A HEAVY-BOTTOMED SKILLET, heat the olive oil over medium heat. Add the parcels and brown lightly, turning once, for a few minutes on each side. Transfer the parcels to a baking pan, arranging them in a single layer. Bring the skillet to medium-high heat, pour in the wine and lemon juice, and scrape up the browned bits from the pan bottom. Pour the pan juices over the chicken.

BAKE THE CHICKEN, turning once halfway through, until golden brown, about 30 minutes. Remove from the oven to a warm platter. Return the pan to the stove top over medium-high heat and boil down the pan juices to reduce slightly.

TO SERVE, remove the toothpicks or string and place 2 parcels on each warmed plate. Spoon the juices over the top and serve.

Rosemary-Smoked
Roast Chicken

RECOMMENDED WINE: **Pinot Bianco**
ALTERNATIVE WINE: **Pinot Grigio**

I smoke about a dozen chickens in this manner every summer. They're easy to cook, delicious, a pleasant surprise for most dinner guests, and I never tire of them. They're good hot, room temperature, or cold (the leftovers make an especially good salad), with or without sauce, and they travel well. The best wine match is light and white, as both oak and wine tannins clash with smoked foods, making them seem dried out and a bit harsh.

1 roasting chicken, about 4 pounds

4 bay leaves

1 clove garlic, chopped

9 large fresh rosemary sprigs

1 small onion, peeled but left whole

2 tablespoons olive oil

salt and freshly ground black pepper

1 cup oak or hickory chips, soaked
    in water for at least 30 minutes

SERVES 6

LIGHT A FIRE IN A CHARCOAL GRILL WITH A COVER, using about 40 briquettes.

REMOVE THE CHICKEN FROM THE REFRIGERATOR ABOUT 30 MINUTES BEFORE YOU PLAN TO BEGIN GRILLING IT, rinse it, and pat it dry. Put the bay leaves, garlic, and 1 rosemary sprig in the cavity, close it with the whole onion, and tie the ends of the legs together loosely with kitchen string. Do not prick or otherwise break the skin, now or later—the chicken will be more tender and tasty if it cooks in its own juices. Rub the bird with the olive oil, and sprinkle liberally with salt and pepper.

WHEN THE COALS ARE HOT (usually after about 30 minutes, when they're barely covered with gray ash, and you can hold your hand about 4 inches above them for only 2 or 3 seconds), move them to either side of the grate and place a metal drip pan between the two banks. A disposable aluminum roasting pan is a good choice. Lightly oil the grill rack and place the chicken on it, centering it over the drip pan. Drain the wood chips and scatter them on the coals on either side along with half the rosemary sprigs. Immediately cover the grill and close the dampers halfway, so that some air gets in, but most of the smoke stays inside. After 30 minutes, check the coals, which should still be medium-hot. Add 4 briquettes to each side, and the remaining rosemary, putting 2 sprigs on each side. Re-cover the grill (the chicken will already be quite brown, but not nearly done yet; don't worry) and roast until done, another 45 minutes. To test for doneness, wiggle one of the bird's legs up and down; it should move easily.

TRANSFER THE CHICKEN TO A WARMED PLATTER, cover loosely with aluminum foil, and let rest for 15 minutes before carving.

Country-Style Ribs
with Spinach and Potato Purée

RECOMMENDED WINE: Refosco
ALTERNATIVE WINE: Schioppettino

Friuli, up in the northeastern corner of Italy bordering Slovenia and Austria, is one of the most interesting places to eat in the country because of the diverse cuisines that intersect there—it's really a culinary crossroad. It's also a stronghold of the Slow Food movement, which is dedicated to preserving the varieties and traditions of artisanal food, and one of the most energetic advocates of the area's gastronomic heritage is Guido Lanzellotti, chef-owner of Osteria Altran, in the little town of Ruda. He and head chef Alessio Devidè made this wonderful, succulent dish for me as an example of the local table, basically simple but richly delicious. (I've adapted it for a simpler presentation, with a note on the dinner-party version.) The area is deservedly famous for white wine, but there are a couple of fascinating reds of note, too, like the two above.

2 ½ pounds country-style pork ribs, trimmed
    to uniform length and cut into 4-rib sections
salt and freshly ground black pepper
3 tablespoons sunflower oil
4 tablespoons extra-virgin olive oil
3 fresh rosemary sprigs
2 fresh thyme sprigs
1 cup chopped onion
1 cup chopped celery
1 cup chopped peeled carrots
2 cloves garlic, chopped
3 cups dry white wine
1 ¼ pounds russet or Yukon Gold potatoes,
    peeled and cut into 2-inch chunks
½ cup milk
6 tablespoons unsalted butter
1 pound spinach, well rinsed, tough stems
    removed, and well dried

SERVES 4

ASK YOUR BUTCHER TO CUT THE PORK INTO 4-RIB SECTIONS, each about 4 $\frac{1}{2}$ inches long, and to score them down the back so they can be easily cut apart (or rolled later; see note). Season the pork with salt and pepper. In a large, heavy-bottomed skillet, heat the sunflower oil over medium-high heat. Add the ribs and brown on both sides, about 3 minutes on each side. Remove the ribs from the pan and set aside.

IN A HEAVY-BOTTOMED SAUCEPAN LARGE ENOUGH TO ACCOMMODATE ALL THE MEAT AND VEGETABLES, heat the olive oil over medium heat. Add the rosemary, thyme, onion, celery, carrots, and garlic and sauté until the aroma rises and the vegetables are beginning to color, 3 to 4 minutes. Place the ribs in the pot and add the wine. Let the liquid come to a strong simmer and then turn down the heat to low. Cover and cook slowly for at least 1 hour, adding slightly salted water continuously as the cooking juices reduce. After 1 hour, the liquid should have a dense, silky texture and the meat should be very dark brown.

REMOVE THE RIBS AND KEEP THEM WARM. Strain the cooking juices into a small saucepan and taste, adding salt if necessary. Cover to keep warm. Discard the herbs and vegetables.

PLACE THE POTATOES IN A LARGE SAUCEPAN AND ADD LIGHTLY SALTED WATER TO COVER BY 1 INCH. Bring to a boil and cook, uncovered, until tender when pierced with a knife tip, 15 to 20 minutes. Drain and cover. In a small saucepan, heat together the milk and 4 tablespoons of the butter over low heat until the butter melts. Pass the potatoes through a ricer or food mill held over the pan. Slowly add the warm milk-butter mixture while whipping the potatoes with a fork, and then continue whipping until the potatoes are creamy. Keep warm.

IN A LARGE SKILLET, melt the remaining 2 tablespoons butter over medium heat. Add the spinach and quickly sauté just until wilted, about 2 minutes.

TO SERVE, reheat the pan juices. Divide the spinach evenly among warmed plates, placing it to one side. Divide the potatoes among the plates as well, placing them on the other side. Lay the ribs in the middle, overlapping both vegetables. Pour the warm pan juices liberally over the pork. Serve at once.

NOTE: *In the restaurant, Guido folds the ribs into a crown, secures the shape with string, and browns and braises them that way. He then stands the crown up on the bed of spinach, fills the inside cavity with mashed potatoes, and pours the pan juices around the edges. Diners cut down the sides of the ribs, which emerge covered with the mashed potatoes. It's an attractive, whimsical presentation, worth doing for a dinner party.*

Central : Tuscany, Umbria, Lazio

Often when people think of Italy, they're thinking of Tuscany—and for good reason. Pisa's tower leans there, the country's prettiest intact medieval walled city is the small gem of Lucca, and Siena is not only a beautifully preserved center of art and history, but also home to the brutal excitement of the famed Palio, the hard-fought bareback-horse race around the central piazza (where, packed in with thousands of screaming locals, my wife learned to swear in Italian without knowing it). The ancient towers of San Gimignano draw hundreds of thousands of visitors every year to the tiny town, and, of course, everybody goes to Florence, the city of the Medicis, Machiavelli, and Dante. Less imagination has gone into Tuscany's kitchens. The food tends to be somewhat rustic, often simply prepared, but at least quite flavorful, based on game or tender slabs of beef or pork, dressed with excellent olive oil and showered with herbs.

Umbria, to the south, has been called "the green heart of Italy." Everything seems to grow there, including an abundance of fruits and vegetables, and its light and fragrant olive oil is now recognized as some of Italy's best. Chocolate from its ancient capital, Perugia, is esteemed all over the world, but the region is most famous for the diversity and well-defined flavors of its cured hams, sausages, and salamis. Perhaps that's a scattered assortment of "bests," but the rest of Umbria's food isn't far behind.

Lazio is essentially Rome, though it spreads a long way along the coast to the north and south of that fabled city, and the peaceful hills around the lakes to the north seem as if they're on another, much quieter planet. Still, the energy, the enthusiasm for the local football team, and the style are based around the idea of Rome, vibrant and lively. The food is elevated peasant food, nothing going to waste, often mixed, fried, adorned with an amazing variety of vegetables, and consumed with gusto.

Most of the wine story in central Italy is Tuscany, however. Its wine families have been in business for more than six hundred years, weaving themselves into Italy's history, and are still active. On a commercial basis, Tuscany leads the way for Italian wine around the world, with Chianti almost a brand name in itself.

But for quite a while, at least in modern times, recognition didn't always mean respect. As the market leader, Chianti was subjected to adulteration by quick-buck operators, as well as pretty terrible imitations (including some horrors from California, stealing the name for raisined, sweet wines). In the 1960s, when Italian wine laws were rewritten and the winemaking began to be upgraded, intelligent reevaluation didn't always extend to Tuscan grapevines. Certainly, in the Chianti zone, vineyards were often replanted without really being upgraded, in a quest driven more by quantity than quality. While other areas in Italy began to surge forward, Tuscany lagged. Critics and the public noticed, and vintners responded with another round of much more organized replanting of better types of grapes, at last giving winemakers something good to work with. The reputation of Chianti was finally restored, and has soared further since.

The result has been an influx of investment, a quickening sense of excitement, and a continuing, eager willingness to experiment. This raging modernity has been a mixed bag, however. Wineries have joined the Chardonnay stampede, for example, and many have also produced expensive Bordeaux-style Cabernets and Sangiovese-Cabernet blends with so much of the latter grape included that they're not legally entitled to be called Chianti (they're informally known as Super-Tuscans). All these wines are expensive collectors' items. Many of the Cabernets can stand proudly with the best of Bordeaux, and are often mistaken for them in blind tastings. Are they "Italian"? Good question. The Sangiovese-Cabernet blends are often very, very good, fascinating wines. Are *they* "Italian"? Sort of. Adding to the excitement is the development of new vineyard areas near the coast, in Bolgheri and the Maremma, by some of the biggest names in Italian winemaking, including Antinori, Gaja, Bolla, and several others. On a tasting tour of the Maremma in the mid-1990s, hardly swallowing any of the rough, rustic wines poured, I couldn't wait to leave. Now, having tasted the new generation of Sangiovese-based wines, I can't wait to get back.

Umbria, home of several wines based on Sangiovese, is often an afterthought in many connoisseurs' minds, but it's actually in ferment right now: the climate is fine, soils are good, and vineyard land is more affordable than in Tuscany. Umbria bristles with new wineries, several of which are already rising stars. Lazio, on the other hand, dominated by undemanding locals and tourists visiting Rome, drifts along on a sea of mostly so-so white wine, with only a few ripples of ambition around the edges so far.

Red Wines

Chianti

For a long time, Chianti was one of the most recognizable wines in the world, thanks to its packaging—corny but cute bulbous flasks wrapped in straw. It was cheap and cheery wine, usually light and sharply acidic, perfect to wash down tons of spaghetti and pizza. It was the first Italian wine most people drank, and left behind without too many regrets when we discovered other wines. In the last decade, it has become a wine to come back to, with pleasure.

Chianti is made primarily from Sangiovese. It is Italy's most widely planted red grape, but it produces wines of the most distinction in Tuscany, between the cities of Florence and Siena, on a hilly, rumpled landscape thick with terraced vineyards, olive groves, and forests, the ridges crowned with castles and small towns of ocher stone buildings. Chianti is almost always a blend, though that has begun to change. The "modern" recipe was first mixed by Baron Ricasoli in the mid-1880s, and included some Canaiolo (a light and aromatic red) and a little of either or both of two whites, Trebbiano and Malvasia.

In 1963, when the Chianti producers began their sometimes painful renaissance, the bulbous flasks and cute straw wrapping were the first things to go, replaced by straight-sided bottles and more dignified labels. Wineries also began cleaning up the winemaking, literally, bringing in stainless steel and sanitation. In the mid-1980s, after careful clonal selection sorted out the best grape strains, winemakers increased the amount of Sangiovese and fine-tuned the blends (some wineries went all the way and moved to 100 percent Sangiovese wines). Another modernizing change was to allow the inclusion of a small amount of "foreign" wine, namely Cabernet Sauvignon or Merlot, on the theory that if you're going uptown, you might as well

head for the penthouse, too. In the last few years, there has even been a move to single-vineyard Chiantis, generally splendid wines usually worth their high price.

The ideal is a little fuller than in the past, though it's still a middleweight, with a lovely pronounced aroma of fresh cherries and a fresh earthiness, slightly soft tannin levels providing moderate astringency, a notable dryness, and a nicely savory directness of flavor. It's not as fruity as some other reds, but that can be seen as a welcome change of pace; its crispness keeps you coming back for more. Most wineries now dispense with white wines in their blends, in favor of about 10 percent Canaiolo or some other native variety, like Colorino, that complement and enhance the character of Sangiovese.

There are several zones producing Chianti: Chianti Classico is the heartland, ideal for the wine and with higher official precepts of winemaking. It offers standard versions, single-vineyard bottlings, and well-aged reserve wines, all of them a bit bigger and bolder and more flavorful, as well as capable of further aging (most of the standard versions improve over five to eight years, the reserves for more than a decade). Seven other zones can either call their wines simply Chianti (most do) or attach their regional name, as in Chianti Rufina or Chianti Colli Senesi. They're generally lighter, more ready to drink earlier.

In all its incarnations, Chianti is at least a wine of rustic elegance, often more than that these days, not terribly complex, but vibrant, crisp, and straightforward, with a pleasantly lingering aroma and flavor. It's not a wine for meat that's elaborately sauced or delicate, but goes well with roasted or grilled meats. At La Torre restaurant in Castellina in Chianti, I once misunderstood the menu and ordered a heroic platter of roast duck, pork loin, and rabbit, meant for two enthusiastic eaters. Too embarrassed to admit my mistake, I tucked in. It took a while, but a bracing, refreshing Chianti Classico helped me get through it.

TYPICAL AROMAS AND FLAVORS
Red cherries, dried roses, and mint predominate, with hints of vanilla, spice, and tobacco often found.

TIPS TO SUCCESSFUL MATCHES
WITH CHIANTI

- *The Tuscan specialty, crostini, thin slices of toasted bread rubbed with olive oil and spread with chicken liver, is a perfect match, as is calves' liver and carmelized onions.*
- *Match savory with savory to take advantage of the wine's lingering, palate-cleansing acidity: roast lamb (especially cooked over charcoal), double-thick grilled lamb chops, and thick grilled steak with mushrooms sautéed in butter.*
- *If there's any Chianti left over after dinner, it's a perfect match with some aged cheeses, such as* pecorino romano *(or aged Gouda or Cheddar).*

Morellino di Scansano

Sangiovese is known as Morellino on the southwestern coast of Tuscany, in an area around the town of Scansano. It's warmer there, so the wine tends to be bigger, broader, plumper, and more amiable (but fairly high in alcohol, too, often 14 percent or more). Generally, the family resemblance of aromas and flavors is present—there's usually a little less acidity than in Chianti, and slightly more dense raspberry-jam fruit. It's also less expensive than Chianti, so it's a good alternative for more casual occasions.

Brunello di Montalcino

The minister who married my wife and me evaluates wine by what he calls the "bishop test." He asks himself, "Is this a wine that will impress the bishop when he comes to dinner once a year?" Brunello is definitely a bishop's wine.

More than one hundred years ago, the Biondi-Santi family isolated a distinctive clone of Sangiovese (known as Sangiovese Grosso) that yielded this particularly bold and concentrated wine—Brunello means "little dark one," a reference to the grape. The wine has always been a big, dark one, demanding long aging in barrel and bottle before it would mellow out. Over the years, a cult built up around this wine. This led to high prices, which only increased its cult status, and increased its prices even more. In the 1960s and 1970s, new vineyards and estates were established; now there's a good supply, and some of it is actually affordable, though still expensive.

Whatever differences of opinion arise about the prices, no one disputes that Brunello is a thoroughbred, an aristocrat among the red wines of the world—the usual accolade is "majestic." The grapes grow south of Chianti, up in the rugged hills, but where it's still a bit warmer. The combination of altitude, soil, and sun makes for rich and concentrated flavors. The wine is made from 100 percent Sangiovese Grosso and matured for two years in oak barrels and three in bottles before being sold; reserves are aged another year after that. In the past, the wines were unapproachable for several more years, hard and aloof, but lately they've been made in a more generous, user-friendly style, still tannic enough to age for a decade or more after they're released onto the market, but accessible for those who find it hard to wait.

Rosso di Montalcino

This is a slightly lighter and much cheaper version of Brunello di Montalcino, which has gained acceptance recently as a good introduction to this style. Basically, in theory at least, the best grapes from Montalcino's vineyards go into the Brunello, and the rest are made into Rosso di Montalcino, which is only aged a year in barrel and another in bottle before being sold. Dark and savory, it's invariably best with another year or two of aging after the vintage. People in the wine business used to refer to it as Brunello's kid brother, but it's grown up lately.

TYPICAL AROMAS AND FLAVORS
Cherries, violets, hints of spices like cinnamon and nutmeg, mingled with vanilla, tar, cedar, and sometimes a faint herbal note in the aftertaste.

TIPS TO SUCCESSFUL MATCHES WITH BRUNELLO DI MONTALCINO AND ROSSO DI MONTALCINO

- *When well aged, say fifteen years old, Brunello is a perfect wine for game birds in complex dishes with a touch of sweetness, such as pheasant casseroled with carrot and other root vegetables, or squab with mushrooms and butternut squash.*
- *With Rosso di Montalcino, think muscularity—sirloin steak, roast pork with plenty of garlic and herbs, a mixed grill of meat and sausages over charcoal.*

Vino Nobile di Montepulciano

Tuscany's oldest noble wine, praised for centuries, is also the one that slipped the most over time, its name something of a sad joke until the mid-1980s, when new winemakers began to revive its grapes and reputation. (The name comes from the town at the heart of its vineyard area, on the southern edge of Tuscany, which is also the name of the main red grape of the Abruzzo, a fact that hasn't helped proper recognition either.) It's made from Sangiovese and small amounts of a few other grapes, and can resemble good Chianti in good years, though there is still no consensus about styles, which tend to be all over the place. Worth trying, however, and if you hit a winner, it will be gorgeous.

Rubesco

Technically, the name of the wine is Torgiano Rosso Vigna Monticchio Riserva, but what you often see on wine lists is Rubesco, the brand name of what is a one-wine appellation in the gentle hills of Umbria. This status is a tribute to the winemaking skills of the Lungarotti family, based just outside Torgiano, a town near Perugia named after an ancient watch-tower—the "tower of Janus," the two-faced god of the Romans—that overlooks the vineyards. The wine is a blend of Sangiovese and some Canaiolo, so it has some family resemblance to Chianti, but what makes it unique, other than the soil and climate of Umbria, is that it is aged in very large, old oak casks instead of toasty small barrels, so that it matures without taking on a taste of wood, and then is aged for another decade in bottles before being sold. Fully matured wines at reasonable prices are rare, let alone wines as graceful and elegant as this one.

Sagrantino di Montefalco

Sagrantino is the wild card in Italy's wine deck, a little
bit of a mysterious outlaw, dark and brooding, but with
quite a bit of charm underneath that tough exterior.
No one quite knows where the grape comes from, and
there isn't a lot of it around, but it's well worth making
an effort to find—there's nothing quite like it.
Sagrantino di Montefalco, named for a little town in
southern Umbria, is unblended, dense, and direct,
more lusty and burly than voluptuous, a little bit scary
the first time you taste it, like the first encounter
with rare breast of squab, or chicken with forty cloves
of garlic. But then, once you get over the shock of the
deeply rich taste of its wonderful sweet-and-savory
combination cavorting on your palate, you want to
keep coming back for more. I last drank it with a plate
of pasta covered in an incredibly complex sauce of
tomatoes, mushrooms, meat, and vegetables, and the
whole combination was so good it almost made me
laugh out loud.

(There is also a sweet dessert wine, Sagrantino
passito, made from semidried grapes, intensely concentrated, outrageously delicious, so deeply flavored it
reminds me of Sacher torte, those incredible Viennese
chocolate cakes smeared with apricot jam. It's a dessert
in itself.)

TYPICAL AROMAS AND FLAVORS
*Blackberry jam, tar, expensive leather, a hint of
mixed spices.*

TIP TO SUCCESSFUL MATCHES
WITH SAGRANTINO DI MONTEFALCO
- *Think big.*

White Wines

Vernaccia di San Gimignano

The pretty village of San Gimignano, with its medieval towers and beautiful hilltop views, is a magnet for tourists, and has provided this pleasant, light, and fairly undistinguished wine with a classy image. It's a varietal wine, though it benefits considerably from blending with other grapes. Barrel aging and other modern winemaking techniques also give its flavor a boost. Most useful as an aperitif or where its lightness becomes a virtue, as at lunch.

TYPICAL AROMAS AND FLAVORS
Dried flowers, dried herbs, a hint of almonds.

TIP TO SUCCESSFUL MATCHES
WITH VERNACCIA DI SAN GIMIGNANO
- *Although it's relatively light, Vernaccia has a softness that makes it feel rounded and fuller than it actually is, so it's an especially good companion to pasta dishes.*

Orvieto

Orvieto is a strikingly beautiful city on a high plateau—from a distance at sunset, it looks like the setting for a fantasy film. The local wine, on the other hand, has been nothing much more than ordinary for a long time, a blend of several grapes, with a little bit of green-apple fruit, a touch of crisp acidity, and few other virtues. Modern winemaking brought out a few more subtle charms, but not a lot, and the addition of Chardonnay to the blend gave it body, but also awkwardness. Just at the end of the century, though, salvation may have arrived. One of the grapes in the blend, Grechetto, turns out to be a potential star, and its increasing usage in the blends is beginning to salvage Orvieto's lackluster reputation. It's a thick-skinned grape that contributes some firmness to the wine, and its aroma and flavor are slightly peachy. Grechetto has, in fact, turned out so well that some wineries in Umbria and Tuscany are making it as a varietal wine on its own, as well as continuing to blend it into Orvieto. It's definitely a contender, worth watching out for in the future. Either wine makes a nice, refreshing aperitif, and matches well enough with casual dishes, especially at lunch.

Est! Est!! Est!!!

For many centuries, the legend was better than the wine: In the best-known version of the tale, in AD 1111, an epicurean German bishop on his way to Rome to see the pope sent a young priest on ahead, with instructions to sample the wine at every inn, and to write Est ("It is" in Latin) on the door of every place with good wine. The emissary was so taken with the wine in Montefiascone that he scrawled Est! Est!! Est!!! on the door of the local inn, and the wine got its name and fame. Until very recently, people have been trying to figure out why, as it was one of Italy's blandest wines.

The problem lay, as it so often does, with the choice of grapes: Trebbiano and Malvasia, the boredom twins, tedious by themselves, soporific in tandem. The other problem was Rome, a large and undemanding market always happy with chilled cheap carafe wine. The landscape the wine comes from is among the prettiest in Italy, a two-hour drive north of Rome, close to the southern border of Umbria, in the hills around Lake Bolsena, an extinct volcano holding a deep blue lake that helps modify the climate. It is also good vineyard land, which until recently was simply a large chunk of unfulfilled promise. In the mid-1990s, a few of Italy's best winemakers set up shop there, however. Working with improved clones of Trebbiano blended with other historical grape varieties they're reviving, they have proved that Est! Est!! Est!!! can be an interesting, sprightly wine, a crisp and refreshing aperitif, and a nice match for appetizers and the sort of street food that tastes best eaten standing up.

TYPICAL AROMAS AND FLAVORS
Apples, dried wildflowers, fresh grapes.

Frascati

Frascati is the other side of the coin from Est! Est!! Est!!! The grapes are the same, the blends of them slightly different, from slightly warmer vineyards in the hills just southeast of Rome. The big difference is attitude—there's little striving to improve the wine. To a great extent, anything goes here, as long as the boredom twins of Trebbiano and Malvasia dominate the blends (sometimes, the little bit of whatever else is in there can make a pleasant difference, but you have no way of knowing until you taste it). Most Frascati is mass-produced for the carafes of Rome and other undiscerning markets, its principal virtue being that it's wet, crisp, and fairly refreshing.

TYPICAL AROMAS AND FLAVORS
Orange blossoms, fresh grapes, a hint of almonds in the aftertaste.

TIP TO SUCCESSFUL MATCHES
WITH EST! EST!! EST!!! AND FRASCATI
- *Do as the Romans do, wherever you are, and make light and spicy the key words: garlic-and-clam pizzas, artichoke fritters, grilled chicken wings, and onion rings, as well as crosscultural favorites such as Sichuan food and chicken fajitas.*

Vermentino

Vermentino is Italy's up-and-coming white grape, now being planted in several areas (see also Sardinia, where it's been established longer), including southern Tuscany. It's medium bodied but feels bigger, almost expansive, and has a definite but not sharp acidity, with a fairly persistent aftertaste; the aroma and flavor both suggest a mixture of herbs, a hint of greenness—quite intriguing. While the vines were young and not yet at their best, the grapes were used for blending, and are only now coming out as varietal wines, but worth trying. There's no overall style prevailing, but the possibilities appear to be excellent.

Vin Santo

The best Vin Santo is made in Tuscany, from concentrated grapes, dried when they're off the vine. Trebbiano and Malvasia grapes are harvested and the bunches are hung from barn rafters for several months, until they're shriveled and raisiny. They are then made into wine and aged in small barrels for a few years. Some of the wine evaporates during this time, which concentrates the wine further and oxidizes it, giving it even more of an aged character that can make it seem dry even though it retains a lot of sugar. Its character is wonderfully complex, making it a fine *vino da meditazione;* in other words, a wine that can be sipped quietly by itself after a meal. But it can also be enjoyed in the simplest sort of way, with almond or hazelnut biscotti, the twice-baked hard cookies seen all over northern Italy. They are dunked into a glass of the wine to soften and soak up the flavor, and then munched with great satisfaction between sips.

Central : **Recipes**

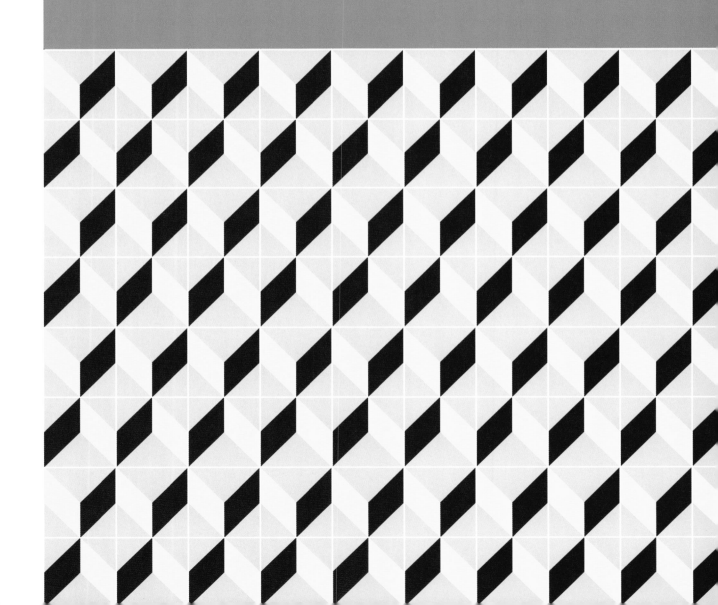

Golden Cod and Eggplant in Pasta Shells

RECOMMENDED WINE: **Est! Est!! Est!!!**

ALTERNATIVE WINE: **Vernaccia di San Gimignano**

Rome is a divided city. It has a cool and elegant aspect and more than its share of wealthy fashionistas mingling with fading aristocracy, but it also has a vividly raffish, genially noisy, garlicky informality, which is the side that is most often reflected in the food. This recipe was created by chef Antonio Martucci, of the International Wine Academy of Rome, and is a perfect example—rich, deeply flavored, and slightly funky. The wine should be well chilled, balancing the food with lightness and refreshment. A crisp green salad is the other perfect accompaniment.

8 ounces salt cod fillet (page 199)

8 ounces *conchiglie* (conch shell–shaped) pasta

4 tablespoons olive oil

good pinch of saffron threads

1 small eggplant, about 8 ounces

1 tablespoon all-purpose flour

2 cloves garlic, chopped

1 red Thai chili, seeded and cut
   crosswise into thin slices

2 tablespoons grated Parmesan cheese

SERVES 2 AS A MAIN COURSE,
OR 4 AS A FIRST COURSE

TWO DAYS IN ADVANCE OF SERVING, begin soaking the cod in fresh water to cover in the refrigerator, changing the water twice a day. At the end of the 2 days, drain the cod and cut into ½-inch pieces, discarding any errant bones. Set aside.

BRING A LARGE POT FILLED WITH SALTED WATER TO A BOIL. Add the pasta, stir well, and cook until nearly done, about 10 minutes. Drain, reserving ½ cup of the cooking water. Rinse the pasta with cold water, drain again, and toss with 1 table-spoon of the olive oil to prevent sticking. Set aside. Add the saffron to the reserved cooking water.

PEEL THE EGGPLANT, cut into ½-inch cubes, and toss the cubes with the flour. (The best way to do this is to put the eggplant and flour in a plastic bag and shake vigorously, then remove the eggplant, shaking off any excess flour.) In a heavy-bottomed skillet, heat 2 tablespoons of the olive oil over medium heat. Add the eggplant and cook, shaking the pan frequently, until it's browned, about 5 minutes. Remove from the pan and set aside, keeping it warm.

IN A LARGE, NONSTICK SAUTÉ PAN OR SKILLET, heat the remaining 1 tablespoon olive oil over medium heat. Add the garlic and chili and sauté until the garlic releases its aroma, about 2 minutes. Add the cod, stir well to coat with the oil, and cook until it begins to brown (don't worry if some of the cubes break up), about 5 minutes. Add the saffron water, stir well, and simmer for another 5 minutes. Add the drained pasta, stir well, and cook for 3 minutes longer, to finish cooking the pasta and blend the flavors. Remove from the heat and stir in the cheese. Add the eggplant and toss well; the pasta shells should partly fill with the sauce.

DIVIDE THE PASTA AMONG WARMED SHALLOW BOWLS AND SERVE IMMEDIATELY.

Tossed Salad in a Basket of Cheese

RECOMMENDED WINE: Vernaccia di San Gimignano
ALTERNATIVE WINE: Orvieto

At Villa Lucia, a luxurious country-house hotel and cooking school just south of Lucca in Tuscany, chef and teacher Giancarlo Talerico starts off his weekly class with a welcoming buffet, and this striking dish is always part of it. While the students admire it, he makes a point of telling them they'll have it again, since it begins the first lesson. Most of them can't believe they'll do it right, but it's easy, and of course even if it isn't quite perfect, it still looks dramatic. The cheese basket should be thin and may have a few holes in it, so whatever goes in shouldn't be too wet or hot, and it will taste a bit salty, so the filling should be fairly mild. Giancarlo's simple dressing is wine friendly; a cool, crisp white is ideal.

8 ounces Parmesan cheese, grated

2 Boston, red-leaf, or other soft-leaved heads lettuce, or one of each, separated into leaves

3 tomatoes, peeled, seeded, and diced

1 red onion, cut in half from top to bottom and then thinly sliced

¼ cup pine nuts

DRESSING:

1 tablespoon honey

juice of 1 lemon

1 small clove garlic, minced

6 tablespoons olive oil

salt and freshly ground black pepper

Parmesan cheese shavings for garnish

SERVES 4

TURN 4 ROUND-BOTTOMED CEREAL OR MIXING BOWLS UPSIDE DOWN ON A WORK SURFACE. To make the baskets, heat a nonstick frying pan at least 8 inches in diameter over medium-low heat. Scatter one-fourth of the grated cheese in a circle on the bottom of the pan and even it out with a nonstick spatula or the back of a fork. It should be thin, no more than $1/8$ inch thick, and cover the bottom of the pan. Tidy the edges with a nonstick spatula, which will make it easier to remove. Watch it carefully; the disk of cheese will bubble at first, then nothing will happen for a few minutes, then it will start to change color. Remove it as soon as it becomes golden (it will take about 4 minutes, and it will continue to cook off the heat). Turn the pan upside down over a bowl and scrape around the edges of the disk with the spatula. The cheese should fall off the pan onto the bottom of the bowl. Protecting your hand with a glove or a piece of paper towel, gently mold the cheese onto the bottom of the bowl and leave on the bowl to cool and firm up, about 5 minutes. Repeat to make 3 more baskets. Set the baskets aside.

TEAR THE LETTUCE LEAVES INTO BITE-SIZED PIECES AND PLACE IN A BOWL. Add the tomatoes, onion, and pine nuts.

TO MAKE THE DRESSING, whisk together the honey, lemon juice, and garlic, then whisk in the olive oil. Season with salt and pepper.

DRIZZLE THE DRESSING OVER THE SALAD AND TOSS LIGHTLY. Place each basket on a plate and fill with the salad. Top with shavings of Parmesan and serve at once.

NOTE: *Almost anything fairly soft and not salty makes a nice addition to the salad: a spoonful of cannellini beans, chunks of cold crabmeat or grilled tuna, squid rings, avocado cubes, or whatever you fancy.*

A Variation and a Snack: Fabulous *Frico*

Good cooking knows no boundaries, and over in Friuli, there are two similar, but tantalizingly different, dishes made much the same way as the recipe at left. (I include them here in fairness to gastronomy rather than geography.) The first time I encountered the crispy cheese snack known as *frico* was at a tasting of Friulian wine, and if it hadn't been a public occasion, I would have eaten them all—they're completely irresistible. Both soft and crispy versions are made in Friuli, sometimes incorporating vegetables, as in a frittata; sometimes in a basket for food, as with the previous recipe; and often by themselves. *Montasio,* the traditional cheese used for these recipes, is saltier than Parmesan, so the wines need to be a bit sturdy and tart, such as Tocai Friulano or Sauvignon Blanc.

TO MAKE SALAD BASKETS, grate 8 ounces aged *Montasio* cheese into a bowl and mix in 1 scant teaspoon all-purpose flour. Make the baskets as directed. *Montasio* melts more quickly than Parmesan, however, so the disk should be turned over once, after about 2 or 3 minutes, and cooked for 1 more minute on the second side. The cheese has a higher fat content than Parmesan, so the disk should slide around easily. Invert onto bowls, let cool, and fill with the same sort of salad.

TO MAKE DELICIOUS SNACKS, grate 8 ounces *Montasio* cheese, omit the flour, and place small piles of the cheese (about 2 tablespoons each) in a nonstick pan over medium-low heat, quickly evening them out with the back of a fork into thin rounds. Shake the pan from time to time, and turn the rounds over after they've begun to melt. You should be able to make 3 or 4 at a time, and get 10 to 12 from this quantity. When they're golden brown on both sides, about 2 minutes on each side after they begin to melt, they're ready. Let cool on racks and serve at room temperature.

Panzanella

RECOMMENDED WINE: **Orvieto**
ALTERNATIVE WINE: **Grechetto**

This wonderful dish, a typical Tuscan bread salad, is a summer staple at my house, perfect as a first course on a warm day. It is definitely handmade, and all the better for it. This recipe is from La Cantinetta Antinori restaurant in Florence, where the Antinori family has been producing wine since 1385. The bread should be firm and dense, not too airy or with large holes; sourdough and *ciabatta*, for example, will not work, but just get mushy. As with all simple dishes, the ingredients should be the best possible, especially the tomatoes.

8 ounces day-old coarse bread,
  cut into thick slices
2 tablespoons red-wine vinegar
6 tomatoes, diced
5 tablespoons coarsely chopped fresh basil
1 small red onion, quartered and thinly sliced
1 yellow bell pepper, seeded, deribbed,
  and cut into ½-inch dice
6 tablespoons extra-virgin olive oil
salt and freshly ground black pepper

SERVES 4

TRIM THE CRUSTS FROM THE BREAD, and cut the bread into 1-inch cubes. Place the cubes in a bowl and dampen them well by sprinkling and then tossing with cold water. They should be quite moist, but not soggy. Squeeze the water out and place the bread in a large bowl. Drizzle with 1 tablespoon of the vinegar, and then add the tomatoes, basil, onion, and bell pepper. Dress with the remaining vinegar and the olive oil, then season with salt and pepper. Mix thoroughly but lightly.

COVER THE BOWL AND REFRIGERATE FOR 30 MINUTES, just enough for a light chill, then serve.

NOTE: *Like any salad, this is adaptable to seasonal vegetables and your taste. Julienned carrots or early season English peas can add some sweetness, while diced cucumbers can provide a nice crunch.*

Leek and Ricotta Pie
with Chickpea Sauce

RECOMMENDED WINE: **Vernaccia di San Gimignano**
ALTERNATIVE WINE: **Vermentino**

These individual pies are a staple in Lucca, delicious but surprisingly easy to make. In the autumn, you also often see them made with fresh porcini. Either way, they make a perfect antipasto, rich but not heavy, very satisfying. They also work as a light lunch with a green salad, or as a first course for dinner, and they are perfect for entertaining: the filling can be made ahead up to 2 hours and refrigerated, then it's just a matter of assembling the pastries and popping them into the oven when the time comes.

> 2 tablespoons olive oil
>
> 4 leeks, white part only, cut in half lengthwise,
>   then cut crosswise into 1/2-inch pieces (4 cups)
>
> 1 tablespoon chopped fresh thyme
>
> 1 cup ricotta cheese
>
> 2 large eggs, beaten
>
> salt and freshly ground black pepper
>
> 1 pound frozen puff pastry, thawed
>   according to package directions
>
> 2 cups Chickpea Sauce, Lucchese Style (page 197)
>
> 2 tablespoons minced fresh chives

SERVES 4

PREHEAT THE OVEN TO 400°F.

IN A HEAVY-BOTTOMED SKILLET, heat the olive oil over medium heat. Add the leeks and thyme and cook, stirring often, until the leeks are soft but not browned, about 10 minutes. Remove from the heat and set aside to cool.

PUSH THE RICOTTA THROUGH A SIEVE PLACED OVER A LARGE BOWL. (This breaks it up and lightens it.) Add most of the beaten eggs, reserving about 2 tablespoons, and then beat together the ricotta and eggs. Add the leeks and mix well. Season lightly with salt and pepper.

ON A LIGHTLY FLOURED WORK SURFACE, roll out the puff pastry about 1/4 inch thick. Cut out 8 rounds, 4 rounds of about 4 inches in diameter, and 4 slightly larger rounds, to overlap the filling. Set out the smaller pastry rounds and spoon one-fourth of the ricotta mixture on each, leaving about a 1/4-inch border around the edge. With a brush or a fingertip, dampen the edge of each pastry round and lay a larger round on top. Pinch the edges shut. Brush the tops of the pastries lightly with the remaining beaten eggs.

PLACE THE PASTRIES ON A BAKING SHEET AND BAKE UNTIL GOLDEN BROWN, about 20 minutes. Just before they are ready, in a small saucepan, heat the Chickpea Sauce over medium heat until hot.

TO SERVE, pour 1/2 cup of the sauce onto each of 4 warmed plates and place a pie on top. Sprinkle chives around the pies.

Arugula, Fontina, and Prosciutto Frittata
with Tomato Essence

RECOMMENDED WINE: **Frascati**

ALTERNATIVE WINE: **Grechetto**

Of all the different omelets in the world, I think frittatas are the sexiest: they come out crispy and brown on the outside, soft on the inside, and lend themselves to more interesting fillings than their counterparts. They're as good at room temperature as they are hot, and since the ratio of egg to filling is low, they're also very wine friendly. This one, lightly salty and peppery, simply needs a refreshing companion, best personified by a crisp Frascati, the Roman's favorite quaff. Grechetto would make for a slightly softer and fruitier companion.

4 large eggs, lightly beaten

2 tablespoons olive oil

1 small onion, minced

3 ounces prosciutto, chopped

3 ounces arugula, tough stems removed
  and roughly chopped

4 tablespoons Tomato Essence (page 198)

2 ounces Fontina cheese, cut into ¼-inch cubes

3 tablespoons grated Parmesan cheese

SERVES 4 AS A MAIN COURSE,
OR 8 AS A FIRST COURSE OR SNACK

PREHEAT THE BROILER.

PLACE THE EGGS IN A LARGE BOWL. In a large, flameproof skillet, heat the olive oil over medium heat. Add the onion and cook, stirring often, until it begins to soften, about 5 minutes. Add the prosciutto and cook, stirring, for another 2 minutes. Remove from the heat. With a slotted spoon, transfer the onion-prosciutto mix to the eggs. Stir in the arugula.

RETURN THE PAN TO MEDIUM HEAT AND POUR IN THE EGG MIX. Let cook until the bottom begins to set, 2 to 3 minutes, and then run a knife around the edge of the eggs to loosen the frittata. When the eggs are set but still liquid in the middle, sprinkle the Tomato Essence over the top, scatter the cubes of Fontina over the top, and then sprinkle the top with the Parmesan.

PLACE THE PAN UNDER THE BROILER ABOUT 4 INCHES FROM THE HEAT, and broil until the cheese melts and the top begins to brown, about 2 minutes. Remove from the broiler and slide the frittata from the pan onto a plate. Serve hot, warm, or at room temperature.

Spicy Spaghetti Carbonara

RECOMMENDED WINE: **Frascati**
ALTERNATIVE WINE: **Est! Est!! Est!!!**

Spicy food and creamy sauces present a challenge to many full-bodied wines, but light, fresh wines can dance nimbly along the tightrope of richly flavored dishes. Frascati is a perfect example. Its delicate overtones of fruit and mildly crisp finish set up your palate for the next bite. Est! Est!! Est!!! is a little more acidic, ending with a light bite that also nicely supplies the required refreshment.

4 large eggs

½ cup grated Parmesan cheese

2 tablespoons minced fresh parsley

1 red Thai or serrano chili, seeded and
    chopped, or ¼ teaspoon dried chili flakes

1 teaspoon freshly ground black pepper

2 tablespoons olive oil

3 cloves garlic, peeled but left whole

4 ounces pancetta, roughly chopped

¼ cup dry white wine

1 pound spaghetti

SERVES 4 AS A MAIN COURSE,
OR 8 AS A FIRST COURSE

IN A LARGE BOWL, lightly beat the eggs. Add the Parmesan, parsley, chili, and pepper and mix together well. Set aside.

IN A SKILLET, heat the olive oil over medium heat. Add the garlic cloves and cook until golden and fragrant, a few minutes. Remove and discard the garlic cloves. Add the pancetta to the skillet and cook until it just begins to brown. Add the wine, bring to a boil, and boil for about 2 minutes, stirring and scraping the pan bottom to loosen the browned bits. Remove from the heat and set aside.

BRING A LARGE POT FILLED WITH SALTED WATER TO A BOIL. Add the pasta, stir well, and cook until al dente, about 11 minutes. Drain and immediately add to the egg mixture, stirring vigorously to coat the pasta completely and create a silky sauce.

QUICKLY REHEAT THE PANCETTA AND WINE, add to the pasta, and stir well again. Divide among warmed shallow bowls and serve immediately.

Pasta Salad with Grilled Eggplant, Minted Peas, and Toasted Walnuts

RECOMMENDED WINE: **Orvieto**
ALTERNATIVE WINE: **Vernaccia di San Gimignano**

I had a dish like this on a hot day in Orvieto, at a sidewalk restaurant down a narrow alley near the magnificent cathedral. It was a weekend near Easter, the lovely town was crowded, and my wife and I were footsore and weary and didn't expect much. This dish, the essence of spring, was sheer serendipity, fresh and bright and delicious. We drank the local wine, our two-year-old son flirted with an Italian girl his age, and everything was all right again.

2 small globe eggplants, about 8 ounces each,
    cut crosswise into ½-inch-thick slices

½ cup olive oil

1 cup walnut halves

1 ½ cups water

8 fresh mint sprigs

1 ½ cups shelled English peas or frozen petite peas

⅓ cup extra-virgin olive oil

grated zest and juice of 1 lemon

1 pound penne or other short tubular pasta

3 tablespoons chopped green onions,
    including light green parts

SERVES 4 AS A MAIN COURSE,
OR 6 AS A FIRST COURSE

LIGHT A FIRE IN A CHARCOAL GRILL, or preheat the broiler. When the coals are hot (usually after about 30 minutes, when they're barely covered with gray ash and you can hold your hand about 4 inches above them for only 2 or 3 seconds) or the broiler is ready, brush the eggplant slices on both sides with the ½ cup olive oil. Place on the grill rack or on a broiler pan lined with aluminum foil and grill or broil about 4 inches from the heat source, turning as necessary, until evenly browned and tender, about 5 minutes per side. Set aside to cool, then cut into 1-inch squares.

IN A DRY SKILLET, toast the walnuts over medium heat, shaking the pan often, until they are fragrant and beginning to take on color, 2 to 3 minutes. Remove from the heat before they darken too much, as they'll continue cooking off the heat, and pour onto a plate. Set aside. (Alternatively, spread the walnuts on a small baking sheet or pan and toast in a 350°F oven until fragrant and beginning to take on color, about 5 minutes.)

IN A SAUCEPAN, combine the water and 4 of the mint sprigs and bring to a boil over high heat. Add the peas, reduce the heat to medium, and simmer just until tender, 2 to 3 minutes. Drain and discard the mint. Set the peas aside.

IN A SMALL BOWL, whisk together the extra-virgin olive oil and the lemon zest and juice to make a dressing. Set aside.

BRING A LARGE POT FILLED WITH SALTED WATER TO A BOIL. Add the pasta, stir well, and cook until al dente, about 12 minutes. Drain, rinse with cold water, and drain again.

IN A LARGE BOWL, combine the pasta, eggplant, peas, green onions, and dressing. Strip the leaves from the remaining 4 mint sprigs, tear each leaf in half, and add to the bowl along with the walnuts. Toss well and serve.

Stuffed **Mussels**

RECOMMENDED WINE: Vernaccia di San Gimignano
ALTERNATIVE WINE: Orvieto

With the longest coastline in Europe, Italy never lacks for shellfish, and mussels (*cozze* in Italian) are on the menu everywhere. This version, a family favorite from Adolfo Folonari, of the Ruffino wine estate in Tuscany, is excellent year-round, but is especially appealing in the winter, when its robust flavor brightens up the chilly grayness. The wine needs to be crisp, with a touch of fruitiness, but not overly serious.

2 ½ pounds mussels

½ cup dry white wine

1 cup dried bread crumbs

½ cup olive oil

½ cup tomato purée

1 small clove garlic, minced

4 tablespoons chopped fresh parsley

pinch of dried chili flakes

5 tablespoons grated Parmesan cheese

SERVES 4 AS A FIRST COURSE,
OR 2 AS A MAIN COURSE

SCRUB THE MUSSELS WELL UNDER RUNNING COLD WATER AND REMOVE THEIR BEARDS, if necessary. Discard any that do not close when tapped. Place the mussels in a large pan, add the wine, cover, and place over high heat. Cook, shaking the pan occasionally, until all the mussels are open, 6 to 9 minutes. Uncover and, with a slotted spoon, remove the mussels to a large bowl, discarding any that do not open. Strain the cooking liquid through a fine-mesh sieve into a small bowl and set aside. Remove the top shell from each mussel and discard.

PREHEAT THE BROILER. Line a large roasting pan with aluminum foil.

TO MAKE THE STUFFING, in a bowl, combine the bread crumbs, ¼ cup of the olive oil, the tomato purée, garlic, parsley, and chili flakes and stir well. Stir in the strained liquid. Cover each mussel with an equal amount of the filling, pressing it in lightly. This is best done with your hand. Arrange the stuffed mussels in a single layer in the prepared pan. Sprinkle each stuffed mussel with about ½ teaspoon of the Parmesan cheese, and then drizzle with a thread of the remaining olive oil. Place the roasting pan under the broiler about 4 inches from the heat source, and broil until the stuffing is browned, about 8 minutes. Divide among plates and serve immediately.

Roast **Pork Loin** *Arista*

RECOMMENDED WINE: **Brunello di Montalcino**
ALTERNATIVE WINE: **Rosso di Montalcino**

Legend has it that this boneless pork roast got the name *arista,* a word used exclusively in Tuscany, when the Tuscan archduke held a banquet in honor of the Greek patriarch. After being served this dish, the guest exclaimed his delight with the Greek *aristos,* a praise of the highest caliber. The Tuscans mangled the pronunciation a bit, but the meaning is there, and the dish is truly exalted. This version is from Castello Banfi, in Tuscany, which has the distinction of being the only winery restaurant in the world to have been awarded a star by the prestigious Michelin Guide.

> 1 boneless pork loin, about 2 pounds, tied
> 4 fresh sage leaves
> leaves from 4 fresh rosemary sprigs
> grated zest of 1 lemon
> salt and freshly ground black pepper
> 3 tablespoons olive oil
> 2 cloves garlic, unpeeled
> ¾ cup dry white wine
>
> SERVES 4

PREHEAT THE OVEN TO 325°F.

MAKE 4 SHALLOW INCISIONS IN THE FAT ON THE TOP AND THEN ON EACH SIDE OF THE MEAT. Finely chop together the sage and rosemary and then combine with the lemon zest and a little salt and pepper, mixing well. Rub the seasoning mixture into the pork, especially into the incisions. Coat the bottom of a roasting pan with 2 tablespoons of the olive oil. Place the roast and the garlic cloves in the pan and drizzle the remaining 1 tablespoon olive oil on top.

ROAST THE PORK, basting and turning halfway through, until it is brown and very tender, about 1½ hours. Turn the roast over again, pour the wine over it, and increase the temperature to 425°F. Continue to roast until the wine evaporates, about 10 minutes. (This last step makes the outside of the meat crispy and enriches the pan juices.) Transfer the pork to a cutting board, cover loosely with aluminum foil, and let rest for 10 minutes.

TO SERVE, thinly slice the pork and arrange on a warmed platter or individual plates. Spoon the pan juices over the slices.

NOTE: *Roasted potatoes are the best accompaniment, especially if they're cooked with the meat: Peel 1 pound waxy potatoes, cut into 1-inch chunks, and drop into boiling water. Cook for 5 minutes and then drain well. When you turn and baste the pork at the halfway point of cooking, add the potatoes to the roasting pan, and shake the pan to coat them with the pan juices. Remove the potatoes from the pan before you add the wine at the end—they should be tender at this point—and keep them warm until serving.*

Grilled Herbed Fish with a *Timballo*
of Zucchini and Pecorino

RECOMMENDED WINE: **Vernanaccia di San Gimignano**
ALTERNATIVE WINE: **Vermentino**

At the Relais La Suvera, a grand hotel in a terraced garden outside Siena in Tuscany, the marriage of food and wine is a family package: the estate grows much of its own produce, and its vineyards are used to produce good organic wine, all of which are served in the hotel's restaurant. The vegetable timbale here is typical of chef Riccardo Setti's approach to combining simple flavors into something more than the sum of its parts. A good alternative fish for this recipe is halibut steak. Boiled potatoes with parsley set off the tangy flavors of fish and vegetables here. The wine should be crisp, cool, and modest, a good supporting player to the flavors of the dish.

2 bone-in monkfish tails, about 1 ½ pounds total

3 tablespoons chopped fresh oregano

2 cloves garlic, chopped

½ teaspoon freshly ground black pepper

4 tablespoons olive oil

3 zucchini, about 1 pound total, cut lengthwise
  into slices ⅛ inch thick

5 tablespoons Tomato Essence (page 198)

3 tablespoons capers, rinsed and chopped

3 tablespoons chopped, pitted green olives

¼ cup grated *pecorino romano* cheese

¼ cup bottled clam juice or fish stock

3 tablespoons chopped fresh parsley

SERVES 4

WORKING WITH 1 MONKFISH TAIL AT A TIME AND USING A SHARP KNIFE, make an incision about ¼ inch deep along one side of the backbone the length of each tail. Make a second incision on the other side of the backbone, turn the tail over, and make 2 more similar incisions. Repeat on the second tail. In a mortar, combine 2 tablespoons of the oregano, the garlic, pepper, and 2 tablespoons of the olive oil and grind together with a pestle to form a paste. (Alternatively, mix together in a small bowl with the back of a spoon.) Rub the paste into both sides of the fish, place the fish on a plate, cover, and refrigerate for at least 1 hour or up to 3 hours.

REMOVE THE FISH FROM THE REFRIGERATOR 30 MINUTES BEFORE COOKING.

PREHEAT THE OVEN TO 400°F.

PLACE THE ZUCCHINI SLICES ON AN OILED BAKING SHEET, brush lightly with the remaining olive oil, and sprinkle with the remaining 1 tablespoon oregano. Place in the oven and bake for 5 minutes. Remove from the oven and let cool. Reduce the oven temperature to 350°F.

LINE FOUR 3 ½-INCH (⅔-CUP) RAMEKINS WITH THE ZUCCHINI SLICES, overlapping them, covering the bottoms and sides, and allowing the ends to hang over the rims. Finely chop any remaining zucchini. In a bowl, combine the chopped zucchini, 4 tablespoons of the Tomato Essence, 2 tablespoons of the capers, 2 tablespoons of the olives, and the cheese and mix well. Divide equally among the lined ramekins. Bring the ends of the zucchini slices over the tops to cover the mix and press down lightly. (These can be assembled in advance for up to 3 hours and refrigerated; bring to room temperature before baking.)

BAKE THE RAMEKINS UNTIL THE TOPS BEGIN TO BROWN AND THE CHEESE MELTS, about 20 minutes.

continued

MEANWHILE, light a fire in a charcoal grill, or preheat the broiler. When the coals are hot (usually after about 30 minutes, when they're barely covered with gray ash and you can hold your hand about 4 inches above them for only 2 or 3 seconds) or the broiler is ready, place the fish on a well-oiled grill rack or on a broiler pan lined with aluminum foil. Grill or broil 4 to 6 inches from the heat source, turning once, until the fish is opaque in the center and firm to the touch, 4 to 5 minutes on each side.

WHILE THE FISH IS COOKING, in a small saucepan, heat the clam juice over medium heat. Add the remaining one tablespoon each capers, olives, and Tomato Essence and the parsley and bring to a simmer. Cook until the liquid is reduced by about one-third, about 10 minutes. Remove from the heat and keep warm. When the fish is ready, transfer it to a cutting board. Cut through the fish down the length of each side of the backbone.

PLACE THE FISH ON WARMED PLATES. Unmold the ramekins by sliding a knife around the edges and turning them over onto the plates. Drizzle the sauce over the fish and serve at once.

Grilled **Chicken Cacciatora**

RECOMMENDED WINE: **Chianti Classico**
ALTERNATIVE WINE: **Rosso di Montalcino**

"Hunter's chicken" has evolved over the years into a rich tomato-based casserole, rather than a savory dish assembled easily from foraging around forest and farmland and cooked in the open air. This version brings it back down to that sort of earthiness with the extra flavor of fire and smoke from charcoal before being finished in a pot.

8 chicken thighs
1 pound carrots, peeled and
    sliced ¼ inch thick
1 onion, chopped
4 tablespoons olive oil
1 pound fresh white mushrooms, sliced
2 cloves garlic, chopped
3 fresh thyme sprigs
salt and freshly ground black pepper
1 cup dry white wine
1 cup Tomato Essence (page 198)
cooked fettuccine, pappardelle, or other
    wide noodles for serving

SERVES 4

LIGHT A FIRE IN A CHARCOAL GRILL WITH A COVER, using about 30 briquettes. Remove the chicken from the refrigerator 30 minutes before cooking. Rinse, pat dry, and trim off excess fat and skin.

IN A BOWL, toss together the carrots, onion, and 2 tablespoons of the olive oil. Place the carrots and onion in the center of a sheet of aluminum foil about 18 inches long. Fold up the sides to enclose completely, and then turn the packet over onto another sheet of foil the same size, again folding up the sides.

WHEN THE COALS ARE HOT (usually after about 30 minutes, when they're barely covered with gray ash, and you can hold your hand about 4 inches above them for only 2 or 3 seconds), move them to either side of the grate and place a metal drip pan between the two banks. A disposable aluminum roasting pan is a good choice. Lightly oil the grill rack and place the chicken thighs on it, centering them over the drip pan. Place the foil packet to one side of the grill, directly over the coals. Cover the grill and cook, turning the foil packet over carefully with a long-handled spatula every 5 minutes for 20 minutes. Remove the packet from the grill and open the foil. Leave the chicken undisturbed until it is nicely browned, 20 to 30 minutes, then remove the chicken from the grill.

IN A LARGE HEAVY-BOTTOMED SAUCEPAN, heat the remaining 2 tablespoons olive oil over medium heat. Add the mushrooms and sauté until they begin to release their juices, just a few minutes. Add the garlic and thyme, and then add the carrots, onion, and chicken, stir well, and season with salt and pepper. Add the wine and Tomato Essence, mix well, and bring to a simmer. Reduce the heat to low, cover, and cook until chicken is completely tender, about 30 minutes.

PUT THE NOODLES IN WARMED SHALLOW BOWLS. Place 2 chicken thighs on top of each portion of pasta and spoon the vegetables and their sauce over them. Serve at once.

Chicken with Green Olives

RECOMMENDED WINE: **Vino Nobile di Montepulciano**
ALTERNATIVE WINE: **Rosso di Montalcino**

Chicken and green olives play nicely off each other, and it often seems that most regions in central and southern Italy have several recipes combining them. This vigorously flavored version is from Benedetta Zaccheo, of the Carpineto winery, an estate in the heart of Tuscany that treads a fine line between tradition and sophistication in admirable style.

1 chicken, about 4 pounds, cut into serving pieces
salt and freshly ground black pepper
3 tablespoons olive oil
2 onions, chopped
1 tablespoon all-purpose flour
2 cups dry white wine
4 large tomatoes, peeled, seeded, and chopped
2 bay leaves
1 tablespoon chopped fresh rosemary
1 tablespoon chopped fresh thyme
1 tablespoon chopped fresh parsley
1 $2/3$ cups pitted green olives
1 pound dried fettuccine

SERVES 6

PREHEAT THE OVEN TO 325°F.

RINSE THE CHICKEN PIECES, pat dry, and season with salt and pepper. In a Dutch oven or other heavy pot large enough to hold the chicken, heat the olive oil over medium heat. Working in batches if necessary, add the chicken pieces and brown well on all sides. Using a slotted spoon, remove the chicken to a plate and set aside.

ADD THE ONIONS TO THE POT AND COOK OVER MEDIUM HEAT UNTIL THEY BEGIN TO BROWN, about 5 minutes. Sprinkle the flour over the onions and stir well to make a thick paste, then add the wine slowly while stirring constantly. Return the chicken to the pot and add the tomatoes, all the herbs, and the olives. Bring to a simmer, cover, and place in the oven. Bake until the chicken is tender, about 1 hour.

JUST BEFORE THE CHICKEN IS READY, bring a large pot filled with salted water to a boil. Add the pasta, stir well, and cook until al dente, about 11 minutes. Drain well.

DIVIDE THE PASTA AMONG WARMED PLATES. Remove the bay leaves from the chicken and divide the chicken and sauce among the plates. Serve at once.

Quick-Braised Quail alla Giancarlo

RECOMMENDED WINE: **Morellino di Scansano**
ALTERNATIVE WINE: **Rubesco**

This was the first of several delicious dishes I ate at Villa Lucia, the well-regarded cooking school near Lucca. When chef-teacher Giancarlo Talerico gave me the recipe, I was amazed at how easy the preparation actually was. Ideally, the birds are served on a bed of polenta and accompanied with "sweet" vegetables, such as English peas or butternut squash.

4 quail

2 cloves garlic

1 tablespoon fresh sage leaves

1 tablespoon fresh rosemary leaves

1/2 teaspoon freshly ground black pepper

salt

4 tablespoons olive oil

2 cups dry white wine

SERVES 2

RINSE THE QUAIL AND PAT DRY. With kitchen scissors, cut the backbone out of each quail. Place the birds, breast side up, on a cutting board and press down to flatten slightly. Insert a skewer across the lower part of each bird, through the thighs and bottom of the breast, to keep them aligned and steady. Chop together the garlic, sage, and rosemary and then combine with the pepper and a little salt, mixing well. Moisten the birds with 1 tablespoon of the olive oil, and rub them well with the seasoning mixture. Place on a plate, cover with plastic wrap, and leave to marinate in the refrigerator for 1 hour.

PREHEAT THE OVEN TO 425°F. Remove the quail from the refrigerator 30 minutes before cooking.

IN A HEAVY-BOTTOMED SKILLET, heat the remaining 3 tablespoons olive oil over medium heat. Add the quail and brown well on both sides, about 5 minutes for each side. Remove to a shallow roasting pan. Add a little of the white wine to the skillet over high heat and deglaze the pan, scraping up the seasonings and browned bits from the bottom. Pour over the quail and then add the rest of the wine to the roasting pan.

ROAST THE QUAIL FOR 8 TO 10 MINUTES FOR MEDIUM-RARE TO MEDIUM. Remove to a warmed plate, and cover loosely with aluminum foil. Put the roasting pan on the stove top over high heat and boil until the sauce is reduced by half, 3 to 4 minutes.

TO SERVE, remove the skewers from the birds and divide the quail between 2 plates. Pour the reduced pan sauce over the top.

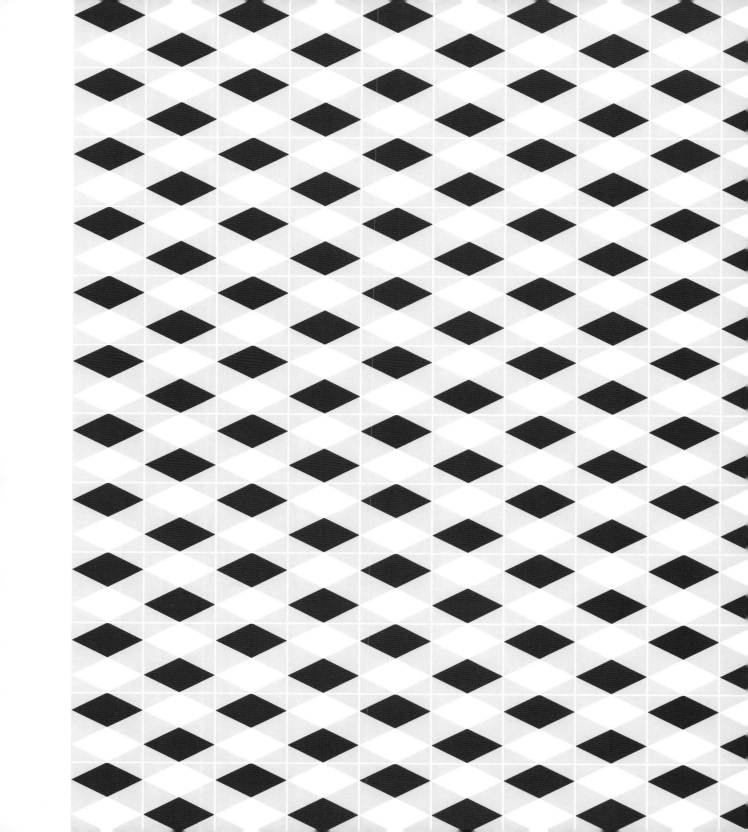

Adriatic : Emilia-Romagna, Marches, Abruzzo, Molise

The regions that stretch down the back of Italy's boot have their cultural and political differences, but they share a defining feature, the Apennine Mountains, which range down their inland flank for hundreds of miles. Emilia-Romagna reaches inland far enough to have a more variable landscape, but the Marches, Abruzzo, and Molise are coastal strips of hills cut by river valleys that tumble down to the Adriatic Sea. Along the shore are fabulous beaches and the only highway, which runs along the little bit of flat space available, right down to Italy's heel. Up in the hills that rise so steeply, every road is a back road, every town is small.

Emilia-Romagna's prosperity is reflected in its rich cuisine and top-quality ingredients: *prosciutto di Parma* ham, *Parmigiano-Reggiano* cheese, unctuous butter, and the increasingly popular seasoning, balsamic vinegar. On the other hand, much of the region's everyday wine is the one-dimensional, dry, light, and sparkling Lambrusco (no relation to the somewhat sweet version of the same name sold in America). It's an oddity, a strange anomaly, especially as the region's more traditional table wines prove they could do more and better.

Down the coast, life is simpler, more down to earth, and so are the wines. I think they reflect the people: straight-forward, unpretentious, and among the most hospitable in Italy. The Marches is sparsely populated and the most divided gastronomically, with a long string of beach resorts down its coast and a rich legacy of fish cookery, contrasted with calorie-laden, well-seasoned country fare in the hills, where truffles and mushrooms thrive. Abruzzo and Molise are poorer, though at least there's an abundance of pasta from wheat grown in the valleys, and of cheese from sheep and cows in the hills. If the rugged mountains keep life to a small scale, they're also beneficial to grapes, providing plenty of surfaces to catch the sun, breezes to keep the grapes clean, and rocky soil that drains well.

Red Wines

Sangiovese di Romagna

Wines from the local version of Italy's most widely planted red grape certainly show a family resemblance to the persistent black cherry flavor of Chianti. For many years, they were thought of as junior cousins, fairly hearty but softer, more straightforwardly easy-to-drink versions of that wine. In the last decade or so, however, winemakers in Romagna have gotten ambitious, and the wines have become more interesting.

In their quest for elegance, some winemakers tried to beef up the wines by aging them in small oak barrels. Others left the pulp, skins, and seeds in the wine for a while after crushing the grapes, which gives the wines body and color but can also make them bitter if carried too far. A few blended in small amounts of Cabernet Sauvignon or Merlot, which deepened the color and added some complexity, but sometimes at the expense of the Sangiovese character. In the last few years, many winemakers have found better balances by simply letting the wines be themselves, medium weight and graceful.

TYPICAL AROMAS AND FLAVORS
Black currants and cherries, hints of plums, occasional spice, sweet tobacco, and cocoa.

TIPS TO SUCCESSFUL MATCHES
WITH SANGIOVESE DI ROMAGNA

- *Remember that the native cuisine is rich, and let that be your guide. Save Sangiovese di Romagna for deeply flavored but relatively rustic and savory dishes, such as lasagna, spaghetti with dense tomato-meat sauce (ragù alla bolognese, named for its hometown), or grilled sausages.*
- *This wine's aromas are subtle, so it doesn't argue with aromatic herbs like thyme, marjoram, or sage.*

Gutturnio

With a name like this, it had better be good. Every time I encounter this wine, I think of the villain in a bad costume movie ("You and the girl can have your freedom, if you survive combat with Gutturnio!"). It's actually a pussycat, a warm, round, amply soft red wine that is a blend of Barbera and Bonarda, a local grape. For a long time, it was simply a staple, one of the everyday wines of Emilia-Romagna and neighboring southern Lombardy, but now the winemakers have awakened to the export market, and the wines are becoming slightly more serious, with some firm tannin and a bit more acidic bite showing up in the latest versions. It's still an undemanding wine that will make you smile, however; hearty and somewhat rustic but not rough—a good companion.

TYPICAL AROMAS AND FLAVORS
Blackberry jam, baked plums, a hint of raisins and mixed spices, with a slight astringent bite in the aftertaste.

TIPS TO SUCCESSFUL MATCHES
WITH GUTTURNIO

- *Its softness and persistent aroma make Gutturnio a good match with easygoing comfort food, such as filled pastas like ravioli or anolini, or a pasta timballo (a molded dish), or buttered green noodles.*
- *The wine also has ideas above its station, and delivers handsomely, making it superb with rich hard cheeses, especially Parmigiano-Reggiano.*

Rosso Conero

The vineyards in the hills above the city of Ancona, the principal city of the Marches, almost run into its suburbs, and if you're driving around the narrow back roads, you can see why grapes have to compete with townspeople: the views of the Adriatic Sea and its sandy beaches are glorious, and the freshening breezes cleanse the air. The wine—Rosso Conero, red from the hills around Mount Conero—is one of Italy's most amiable. It is made mostly from a grape called Montepulciano (not to be confused with the Tuscan town and wine sharing the same name), sometimes with a little Sangiovese blended in. The Montepulciano grape makes inky, dark purple wine. That's usually a sign that the wine will be intense, dense, brooding, and tongue-searingly tannic, but Rosso Conero is actually as easy as a golden retriever puppy, with almost sweet, smooth tannins and a plush texture. Amazingly, it ages well for a soft wine, so that it can easily be drunk young, say, two or three years after the vintage date, or with a little age, perhaps five to seven years old.

TYPICAL AROMAS AND FLAVORS
Elderberries, blackberries, and wild cherries, with hints of tobacco and black pepper.

TIPS TO SUCCESSFUL MATCHES
WITH ROSSO CONERO
- *Don't be taken in by the amiability factor of the wine. It also has enough concentration and personality to pair well with complicated dishes, such as* Vincisgrassi *(page 129) and other types of lasagna, stuffed roast pork, rabbit stew, or chicken casseroles featuring garlic and wine.*
- *The wine's softness makes it good for barbecued and smoked meats, not just for the nice fit of noncompeting flavors, but also for the usual informality of the occasion.*

Montepulciano d'Abruzzo

This is the same grape as the one used in the Marches to the north for Rosso Conero, and much better known as a varietal wine, though not always by consumers: A lot of Montepulciano d'Abruzzo has been exported over the years, but much of it ended up as the anonymous "house wine" in Italian and Italian American restaurants. It has the same aroma and flavor profile and uses as Rosso Conero, but there's a lot more of it, and it's usually very good value.

White Wines

Albana

Glowing descriptions of this wine's virtues date back through the Middle Ages all the way to the fifth century, but modern wine drinkers may well wonder what the fuss was all about. Albana, sometimes still known by its full name, Albana di Romagna, is fairly pleasant, with a faint dried-flower aroma and mildly peachy flavor, and rather acidic. If you find yourself confronting one of the wonderful fish stews made near the coast in Emilia-Romagna, the wine will be at least all right, especially if the other available wine is Trebbiano, which is the really dull other white wine of the region. Anywhere else in the world, and you're sure to have a more interesting choice of alternative wines. (On the other hand, there is a rare sweet version, called Albana *passito,* made from semidried grapes that concentrate the sugar levels, which has some charm as a dessert wine.)

Verdicchio

For generations, Verdicchio was easily recognizable by its bottles, which were green fish-shaped amphoras. The recognition factor helped the wine sell well—"I'm having fish, I guess I'll have that one, it must go with it" was the psychology—but its style was fairly one-dimensional, without a lot of character. Then, along came technology, in the form of stainless-steel tanks that enabled cold, controlled fermentation, and Verdicchio began to come into its own as a lightly fragrant, nicely fruity, tightly tart winner, with genuine character, several virtues beyond refreshment, and a profile suited to more sophisticated fish preparations. (More sophisticated wine drinkers came along, too, when those corny bottles were dropped.) Now, the wine is not only popular, but increasingly respected.

Verdicchio comes in two principal types, each named for its region, and each slightly different in character. The larger area by far, and best known, is Verdicchio dei Castelli di Jesi (Jesi is a town). From a smaller zone, higher in the hills where it's cooler, comes Verdicchio di Matelica, which is a bit more definite in character, a little tighter, and with slightly more depth and strength. Both have clearly defined flavors, with the zippy bite of cool-weather apples like Granny Smiths and an aftertaste of toasted almonds—intriguing.

TYPICAL AROMAS AND FLAVORS

Apples, peaches, quinces, lemon flowers, sometimes a touch of kiwifruit, and slight flavor of almonds in the aftertaste.

TIPS TO SUCCESSFUL MATCHES
WITH VERDICCHIO

- *Its well-defined character and acidity make Verdicchio a good match with some offbeat types of seafood, such as smoked fish, hearty fish stews made without tomatoes, salt-cod dishes and dips, and even old-fashioned fish and chips.*
- *Verdicchio has enough zip to dance with rustic white-meat preparations, such as rabbit braised with fennel or roasted with carrots and other root vegetables, garlicky roast pork loin, or chicken grilled with rosemary.*

Adriatic **:**
Recipes

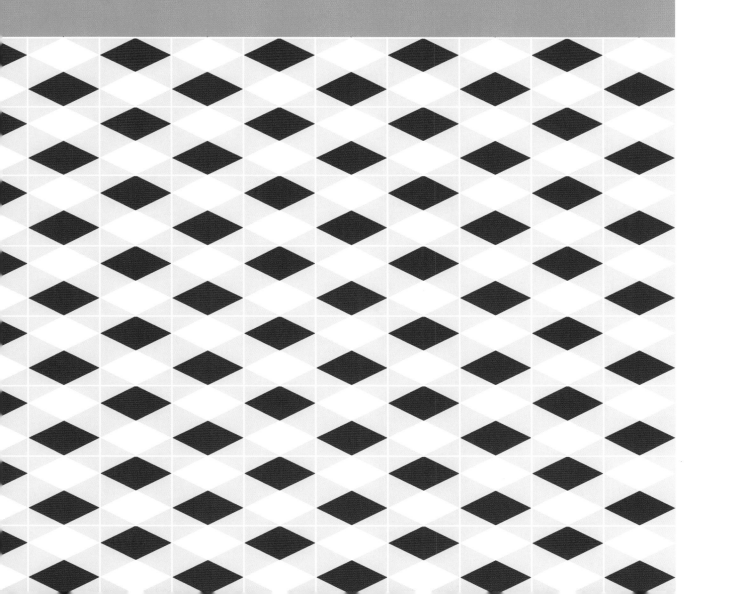

Polenta, Pesto, and Red Pepper **"Terrine"**

RECOMMENDED WINE: **Verdicchio dei Castelli di Jesi**
ALTERNATIVE WINE **Verdicchio di Matelica**

Up in the hills of Montefeltro, high above the Adriatic coast in the Marches, many small towns celebrate the autumn harvest with festivals—chestnuts in one, honey in another, superb pecorino cheese in several, and so on, always with a gloriously smelly trade in truffles on the side. Polenta is a staple, and stout ladies chat and sing while they take turns stirring tubs of the stuff for forty-five minutes and then dish it up with sausages, cheese, mushrooms, or other vegetables. (I've substituted the much easier instant polenta, which still takes some arm power.) It's basic, wonderful food, and it gave me this idea for a superb lunch dish. I have broiled the polenta here, but you can also grill it over a medium-hot charcoal fire, if you are deft at grilling or have a fine-mesh screen or basket to place on the grill rack. Serve the polenta with a green salad and perhaps a grilled sausage on the side, or cut it into smaller rectangles and serve it as part of a buffet.

> 4 large red bell peppers, roasted
> and coarsely chopped (see note)
> 4 ounces fresh goat cheese,
> crumbled into small pieces
> 18 fresh basil leaves, chopped
> 2 tablespoons Pesto (page 196)
> ¼ cup olive oil
> 6 cups water
> 2 teaspoons salt
> 2 cups instant polenta

SERVES 6

PUT THE BELL PEPPERS, goat cheese, basil, and Pesto in 4 separate bowls. Also have a bowl of cold water ready to use for moistening your hands as you assemble the dish. Brush the bottom and sides of a baking pan about 9 inches square and 2 inches deep with a little of the olive oil. In a large heavy-bottomed saucepan, bring the water to a boil and add the salt. Add the polenta in a steady stream, stirring all the while so it doesn't clump. Continue to stir for about 5 to 6 minutes, at which point it will begin to come away from the sides of the pot, which means it's done.

POUR HALF THE POLENTA INTO THE BAKING DISH AND SMOOTH OUT WITH A RUBBER SPATULA AND YOUR HANDS. (Work as quickly as possible, as the polenta thickens as it cools.) Spread the Pesto on the surface, and sprinkle evenly with the peppers, basil, and goat cheese. Spoon the remainder of the polenta over the top and again smooth out, pressing down very lightly. Cover with plastic wrap, set aside to cool, and then refrigerate for up to 2 hours before continuing.

PREHEAT THE BROILER. Cut the polenta into 6 equal pieces, place on a baking sheet, and brush lightly with the remaining olive oil. Place in the broiler 4 to 6 inches from the heat source and broil, turning once, until golden brown, 2 to 3 minutes on each side. Serve immediately.

NOTE: *To roast the bell peppers, preheat the broiler. Cut the peppers in half lengthwise and seed and derib them. Place them cut side down on a baking sheet and place in the broiler 4 to 6 inches from the heat source. Broil until the skins have blackened, 12 to 14 minutes. Remove the peppers from the broiler, place in a paper bag, close the top, and set aside for about 15 minutes to cool. Rub off the skin, then cut as directed.*

Spaghettini with Shrimp and Ginger

RECOMMENDED WINE: **Verdicchio dei Castelli di Jesi Classico**
ALTERNATIVE WINE: **Verdicchio di Matelica**

Susanna Fumi is one of the generation of younger chefs revitalizing Italian cooking, and her award-winning restaurant, Osteria del Vecchio Castello, in Montalcino, is an obligatory stop for anyone touring southern Tuscany. Here, she's created a simple, delicious dish inspired by the seagoing trade between Adriatic seaports and northern Africa. The spiciness is warm rather than hot, and wonderfully aromatic, a perfect counterpoint to the cool white wines of the coast.

1 pound spaghettini, broken into
  4-inch lengths
4 tablespoons olive oil
1 clove garlic, peeled but left whole
pinch of dried chili flakes
12 ounces shrimp, peeled, deveined,
  and cut in half lengthwise
$1/4$ cup chopped fresh parsley
salt
2 tablespoons grated fresh ginger

SERVES 4

BRING A LARGE POT FILLED WITH SALTED WATER TO A BOIL. Add the pasta, stir well, and cook until al dente, about 10 minutes.

JUST BEFORE THE PASTA FINISHES COOKING, in a heavy-bottomed saucepan large enough to accommodate the shrimp and cooked pasta, heat the olive oil over medium heat. Add the garlic and chili flakes and cook until the garlic releases its aroma; do not let it brown. Add the shrimp and parsley and season with salt. Stir well and cook until the shrimp turn pink, about 2 minutes. Remove from the heat. Discard the garlic.

WHEN THE PASTA IS READY, drain it, reserving $1/2$ cup of the cooking water. Add the pasta to the saucepan and toss to combine with the other ingredients. Return to medium heat. Add the reserved cooking water and the ginger and stir thoroughly to combine. Let it heat through, about 1 minute, and remove from the heat.

DIVIDE THE PASTA AMONG WARMED SHALLOW BOWLS AND SERVE IMMEDIATELY.

Epicures' **Macaroni and Cheese** with Truffle Oil

RECOMMENDED WINE: **Rosso Conero**
ALTERNATIVE WINE: **Montepulciano d'Abruzzo**

Every October, the tiny town of Sant'Agata Feltria, high in the mountains of the Marches, swells into a massive street party as thousands of people arrive for the White Truffle Fair. From stalls lining the narrow streets, you can taste wine or buy food, toys, herbs, or wrought-iron furniture; flip through calendars depicting the high points of Mussolini's career; and sample a delicious array of snacks, including sandwiches of cheese drizzled with olive oil infused with aromatic chunks of truffle. The pungent tubers are everywhere, gnarled and stinking wonderfully of earth and musk, expensive but worth the splurge (I paid about sixty dollars for one the size of a walnut and was told I got a good deal). There's no flavor quite like it, and the next best thing to a fresh one is good truffle oil. Besides this recipe, try adding a little to cream soups or mashed potatoes—they become funky, unique, and delicious.

1/3 cup dried bread crumbs

1/3 cup chopped pine nuts

1 ounce dried porcini mushrooms

1 cup boiling water

12 ounces penne or macaroni

3 tablespoons truffle oil

2 1/2 cups shredded Fontina cheese

salt and freshly ground black pepper

1 tablespoon unsalted butter

1 tablespoon all-purpose flour

1/4 cup milk

SERVES 4

IN A SMALL BOWL, mix together the bread crumbs and pine nuts well. Set aside. Put the mushrooms in a small heatproof bowl, pour the boiling water over them, and let soak for about 30 minutes to soften. Remove from the water and rinse under running cold water. Chop finely and set aside. Carefully pour most of the soaking water into a cup, leaving the dregs behind in the bowl. Set aside.

PREHEAT THE OVEN TO 400°F. Butter a 2-quart baking dish.

BRING A LARGE POT FILLED WITH SALTED WATER TO A BOIL. Add the pasta, stir well, and cook until al dente, about 11 minutes. Drain thoroughly and place in a bowl. Add 1 tablespoon of the truffle oil and toss well.

COVER THE BOTTOM OF THE PREPARED BAKING DISH WITH HALF OF THE PASTA. Scatter the mushrooms evenly over the top and then scatter on half of the cheese. Sprinkle with salt and pepper. Put the remaining pasta on top.

IN A HEAVY-BOTTOMED SAUCEPAN, melt the butter over medium heat. Whisk in the flour and cook until it begins to brown, about 2 minutes. Slowly whisk in the milk, and then whisk in the mushroom liquid. Reduce the heat to medium-low and cook, whisking several times, until the mixture thickens, about 5 minutes. Add the remaining cheese and stir until it begins to melt. Pour over the pasta, smoothing any lumps with a fork. Scatter the bread crumb mixture over the top.

BAKE THE PASTA UNTIL THE TOP IS LIGHTLY BROWNED, about 15 minutes. Drizzle the remaining 2 tablespoons truffle oil over the top and bake for 5 minutes more. Remove from the oven and let rest for 5 to 10 minutes before serving.

Vincisgrassi

RECOMMENDED WINE: **Verdicchio**
ALTERNATIVE WINE: **Rosso Conero**

This is a glorious, rich lasagna, usually reserved for celebrations. It's a specialty of the Marches, where truffles are a prized crop, and in the autumn, they're often included in the dish. Sometimes so are luxury meats like sweetbreads, and there are also meatless versions crammed full of several vegetables, each cooked a different way. (If you wanted to crank this one up another notch, you could cut down on the meat sauce and include a layer of sautéed vegetables drizzled with truffle oil.) Although it has a lot of ingredients, the dish is quite easy, just a matter of making an assemblage. The ideal wine is very much a matter of personal choice between white and red, although it should never be too heavy. With a dish like this, it's just an accompanist.

1 ounce dried porcini mushrooms
1 ½ cups boiling water

MEAT SAUCE:
3 tablespoons olive oil
3 ounces pancetta, chopped
2 cloves garlic, chopped
1 onion, chopped
1 carrot, peeled and finely chopped
8 ounces ground veal
8 ounces ground pork
½ cup dry white wine
1 cup reduced-sodium canned beef broth
1 cup tomato purée
1 bay leaf
pinch of ground cinnamon
pinch of freshly grated nutmeg
salt and freshly ground black pepper
6 ounces fresh white mushrooms,
   cut into ¼-inch-thick slices
6 ounces chicken livers, trimmed and chopped

BÉCHAMEL SAUCE:
3 cups milk
½ cup unsalted butter
½ cup all-purpose flour

12 ounces dried lasagna noodles
1 cup grated Parmesan cheese
1 cup grated *pecorino romano* cheese

SERVES 6

continued

PUT THE MUSHROOMS IN A SMALL HEATPROOF BOWL, pour the boiling water over them, and let soak for 30 minutes to soften. Remove from the water and rinse under running cold water. Chop finely and set aside. Carefully pour 1 cup of the soaking water into a measuring cup, leaving the dregs behind in the bowl. Set aside.

TO MAKE THE MEAT SAUCE, in a large heavy-bottomed saucepan, heat the olive oil over medium-low heat. Add the pancetta, garlic, onion, and carrot and cook, stirring, until the pancetta has begun to brown, about 5 minutes. Add the veal and pork, raise the heat to medium, and cook, breaking up the meats with a wooden spoon, until they are lightly browned, about 5 minutes. Pour in the wine and cook until it has almost evaporated. Add the broth, tomato purée, bay leaf, cinnamon, and nutmeg and season with salt and pepper. Stir well, reduce the heat to low, and simmer gently for 45 minutes. Add the reserved porcini, sliced fresh mushrooms, and chicken livers. Cook for 15 minutes longer. Remove from the heat.

TO MAKE THE BÉCHAMEL SAUCE, in a small saucepan, heat the milk over medium-low heat until bubbles form around the edges of the pan. In a medium saucepan, melt the butter over medium heat. Gradually whisk in the flour and continue whisking until the mixture turns a golden color, about 3 minutes. Gradually whisk the hot milk into the flour mixture until smooth. Add the reserved mushroom liquid and continue to whisk until the mixture thickens, 8 to 10 minutes. Cover and remove from the heat.

PREHEAT THE OVEN TO 400°F. Oil a 9-by-13-inch baking dish.

BRING A LARGE POT FILLED WITH SALTED WATER TO A BOIL. Add the pasta, stir well, and cook until al dente, about 8 minutes. Meanwhile, in a bowl, mix together the 2 cheeses.

DRAIN THE PASTA, lay the sheets on a damp kitchen towel, and lay another damp towel over them. Pour a thin layer of béchamel sauce on the bottom of the prepared baking dish. Arrange a single layer of noodles on top. Scatter one-third of the cheese over the noodles. Pour one-third of the meat sauce over the cheese layer and top with a thin layer of béchamel. Repeat twice more, finishing with a layer of béchamel. (You may find you do not use up all the béchamel sauce, but be sure not to leave the top dry.)

BAKE THE LASAGNA UNTIL THE TOP HAS BROWNED SLIGHTLY, about 25 minutes. Remove from the oven and let sit for 10 minutes to set before cutting into squares to serve.

Penne with Mushroom-Olive Cream

RECOMMENDED WINE: **Gutturnio**
ALTERNATIVE WINE: **Sangiovese di Romagna**

Claudio Camisa is an old-fashioned Italian grocer from Parma, now based in Soho, in London, happily commuting back and forth for his import business. Of course, he collects recipes, and after a long lunch one day, he passed along a few to me, several of which immediately became weekend-lunch favorites, especially this one. Choose olives with good flavor, and never presliced or chopped versions. A light red is the best wine match.

2 tablespoons olive oil

1 clove garlic, chopped

12 ounces fresh cremini or
   portobello mushrooms, coarsely chopped

12 ounces penne

1 ¼ cup black olives, pitted and sliced in half

2 tablespoons chopped fresh parsley

4 tablespoons unsalted butter

1 small dried red chili, seeded and chopped

salt

¼ cup mascarpone cheese

4 tablespoons grated Parmesan cheese

SERVES 4

IN A HEAVY-BOTTOMED SAUCEPAN OR SKILLET, heat the olive oil over low heat. Add the garlic and cook until the aroma rises. Add the mushrooms, turn up the heat to medium, and cook, stirring, until they are lightly browned, about 5 minutes. Remove from the heat and allow to cool slightly.

BRING A LARGE POT FILLED WITH SALTED WATER TO A BOIL. Add the pasta, stir well, and cook until al dente, about 11 minutes.

WHILE THE PASTA IS COOKING, place the mushroom-garlic mix, olives, and parsley in a blender or food processor and process with brief pulses, just enough to make a coarse purée. Do not blend too smoothly. In a large heavy-bottomed saucepan, melt the butter over low heat. Add the chili and cook, stirring, until its aroma rises, 2 to 3 minutes. Stir in the olive-mushroom mixture and season with salt. Stir in the mascarpone and let it just heat through; do not let it boil.

DRAIN THE PASTA AND PLACE IN A LARGE WARMED BOWL. Add the olive-mushroom sauce and toss well to coat the pasta thoroughly. Divide among warmed plates and sprinkle each serving with 1 tablespoon Parmesan. Serve at once.

Osso Buco, Emilia-Romagna Style

RECOMMENDED WINE: **Sangiovese di Romagna**
ALTERNATIVE WINE: **Chianti Classico**

Osso buco means "hollow bone" in Italian, and this famed dish is named for the way the marrow shrinks into the central bone of the thick slice of cross-cut veal shank during cooking. The marrow is considered a delicacy, and there's a special slender spoon to scoop out that tidbit, known as a *scavino,* a slang term for "tax man." The classic version, from Milan, doesn't include tomatoes or vegetables, but the version from Emilia-Romagna, which is much richer, does, and I think it's superior. The usual accompaniment is a fairly plain risotto, but creamy olive-oil mashed potatoes suit this version much better. Though white wine is used in the sauce, and the lemon-zest *gremolata* added at the end gives it a citric hint, red wine is the best accompaniment, especially a Sangiovese-based one.

4 pieces veal shank, about 1 ½ pounds total
  and each about 1 inch thick
3 tablespoons all-purpose flour
4 tablespoons unsalted butter
2 tablespoons olive oil
½ cup dry white wine
1 onion, chopped
2 carrots, peeled and chopped
2 stalks celery, chopped
2 cloves garlic, chopped, plus 1 clove roughly chopped
1 tablespoon chopped fresh thyme
salt and freshly ground black pepper
1 cup coarsely chopped, peeled tomatoes
2 cups reduced-sodium canned beef broth
grated zest of 1 lemon
2 tablespoons roughly chopped fresh parsley

OLIVE-OIL MASHED POTATOES:

1 ½ pounds russet or Yukon Gold potatoes,
  peeled and cut into 2-inch chunks
⅓ cup milk
¼ cup olive oil

SERVES 4

continued

DUST THE VEAL SHANK PIECES WITH THE FLOUR, shaking off the excess. In a large heavy-bottomed saucepan, melt 2 tablespoons of the butter with the olive oil over medium heat. Add the veal and brown well on both sides. Remove to a plate. Add the wine to the pan and stir well over medium heat, scraping up any browned bits from the pan bottom. Add the remaining 2 tablespoons butter to the pan along with the onion, carrots, celery, whole garlic, and thyme. Season with salt and pepper, stir well again, and cook until the vegetables just soften, 4 to 5 minutes.

CAREFULLY PLACE THE VEAL SHANKS ON TOP OF THE VEGETABLES. Add the tomatoes and broth and bring to a simmer. Cover, reduce the heat to low, and braise, turning the veal pieces once at the halfway point, until the meat begins to come away from the bones, about 2 hours. Add water to the pan if the juices begin to cook away.

MEANWHILE, finely chop together the lemon zest, parsley, and roughly chopped garlic and set aside.

ABOUT 30 MINUTES BEFORE THE VEAL IS READY, begin preparing the potatoes. Place the potatoes in a large saucepan and add lightly salted water to cover by 1 inch. Bring to a boil and cook, uncovered, until tender when pierced with a knife tip, 15 to 20 minutes. Drain and cover. In 2 small saucepans, heat the milk and olive oil over low heat until warm. Pass the potatoes through a ricer or food mill held over the pan. Slowly add the warm milk while whipping the potatoes with a fork until smooth. Then whip in the warm olive oil, and continue whipping until the potatoes are fluffy.

TO SERVE, place a bed of mashed potatoes on each warmed plate or shallow bowl. Place a piece of veal shank on top, and ladle on some of the cooking juices. Scatter the lemon zest mixture over the veal.

Parmesan Beef with Balsamic Sauce

RECOMMENDED WINE: **Sangiovese di Romagna**
ALTERNATIVE WINE: **Chianti Classico**

For gourmets, Emilia-Romagna is close to heaven: *Parmigiano-Reggiano* is one of the world's great cheeses and *grana padano* is only a few steps behind, Parma ham is considered the best prosciutto, the local butter is sinfully voluptuous, the pasta is made with eggs, and the balsamic vinegar is a revelation, sweetly tart from careful aging. The locals are known as heroic eaters, which makes me wonder which came first, the food or the appetite? Here, the sauce that results from the slow cooking is silky and luxuriant with a little bite, and the wine should match those attributes. A Sangiovese-based bottle is best. Accompany the dish with mashed potatoes, which will make the most of the sauce.

1 flank steak, about 2 pounds

¼ cup balsamic vinegar

½ cup grated Parmesan cheese

3 tablespoons finely chopped fresh rosemary

4 thin slices pancetta or bacon

1 teaspoon freshly ground black pepper

2 tablespoons olive oil

3 carrots, peeled and cut into 2-inch chunks

4 shallots, quartered

3 cloves garlic, peeled but left whole

1 bay leaf

2 cups dry red wine

¼ cup tomato purée

3 tablespoons minced fresh parsley

SERVES 6

PREHEAT THE OVEN TO 325°F.

PLACE THE STEAK ON A CUTTING BOARD WITH THE GRAIN OF THE MEAT RUNNING IN THE DIRECTION YOU ARE FACING. Butterfly the steak by slicing it horizontally from right to left, cutting nearly all the way through. Open it out like a book and lightly pound it flat with a mallet, rolling pin, or the bottom of a skillet. Brush the balsamic vinegar liberally over the cut surface and allow it to stand for a few minutes to soak in. Sprinkle the cheese as evenly as possible over the surface, and then the rosemary. Lay the pancetta slices on top, running them with the grain of the meat. Sprinkle with pepper. Working from the edge closest to you, roll up the meat and tie with kitchen string at 2-inch intervals.

IN A DUTCH OVEN OR OTHER HEAVY POT, heat the olive oil over high heat. Add the meat roll and brown on all sides, about 10 minutes total. Add the carrots, shallots, garlic, bay leaf, wine, and tomato purée, cover, place in the oven, and braise, turning and basting every 30 minutes with the pot juices, until very tender, 2 ½ to 3 hours. (Add water to the pot if the juices begin to cook away.)

REMOVE THE MEAT ROLL FROM THE POT, place seam side down on a cutting board, and snip the strings. Cover loosely with aluminum foil and let rest for 10 minutes. Remove the bay leaf from the pot juices and discard, then reheat the juices on the stove top. Cut the meat crosswise into 1-inch-thick slices and arrange the slice, cut side up so that the pattern of the roll shows, on warmed plates. Spoon the warm pan juices over the slices. Garnish with the parsley and serve.

Grilled **Stuffed Pork Tenderloin** with Vegetables

RECOMMENDED WINE: Rosso Conero
ALTERNATIVE WINE: Montepulciano d'Abruzzo

Pork takes readily to the grill, but its savoriness also makes it a mouth-filling natural partner for wine. In this preparation, with a variety of herbs in play and a bit of zing from the peppers and balsamic, a good light red will carry the generous flavors along.

4 tablespoons olive oil

1 tablespoon chopped fresh tarragon

2 zucchini, about 8 ounces total,
    cut on the diagonal into 1-inch chunks

1 globe eggplant, sliced crosswise
    into ½-inch-thick rounds

8 ounces fresh portobello mushrooms,
    cut in half through the stem and then
    each half cut vertically into ½-inch slices

1 tablespoon finely chopped fresh rosemary

salt and freshly ground black pepper

1 red bell pepper, seeded, deribbed, and chopped

1 tablespoon chopped fresh sage

1 clove garlic, chopped

1 shallot, chopped

1 tablespoon balsamic vinegar

2 pork tenderloins, about 1 pound each

1 pound dried tagliatelle

3 tablespoons unsalted butter

SERVES 4

IN A LARGE BOWL, combine 2 tablespoons of the olive oil and the tarragon. Add the zucchini, eggplant, and mushrooms and toss well to coat. Set aside to marinate.

IN A SMALL BOWL, whisk together 1 tablespoon of the olive oil, the rosemary, and a little salt and pepper. Set aside.

IN ANOTHER SMALL BOWL, mix together the bell pepper, sage, garlic, and shallot. In a small skillet, warm the remaining 1 tablespoon olive oil over medium-low heat. Add the bell pepper mixture and cook, stirring, until the aroma rises, about 5 minutes. Remove from the heat, let cool, and add the balsamic vinegar. Stir to mix well.

LIGHT A FIRE IN A CHARCOAL GRILL WITH A COVER, using about 30 briquettes.

BUTTERFLY THE TENDERLOINS BY MAKING A DEEP SLIT DOWN THE LENGTH OF EACH ONE, cutting nearly all the way through. Open them out like a book and flatten a bit by pressing down firmly on the meat. Spoon the bell pepper mixture along the middle of each tenderloin, dividing it evenly. Bring the sides together and secure the meat closed, tying with kitchen string at 2-inch intervals. Brush the rosemary mixture evenly over the outside of the tenderloins. Cover and set aside.

WHEN THE COALS ARE HOT (usually after about 30 minutes, when they're barely covered with gray ash and you can hold your hand about 4 inches above them for only 2 or 3 seconds), move them to either side of the grate and place a metal drip pan between the two banks. A disposable aluminum roasting pan is a good choice. Remove the zucchini, eggplant, and mushrooms from the bowl and place on double layers of paper towels to drain any excess oil. Place the tenderloins in the middle of the grill, centering them over the drip pan. Cover and cook for 15 minutes. Turn the tenderloins over onto their other side, re-cover, and cook until browned, about 10 minutes. Remove the pork to a warmed platter and cover loosely with aluminum foil. Place the vegetables directly over the coal banks and grill, turning once, until nicely browned and tender, about 4 minutes on each side.

MEANWHILE, bring a large pot filled with salted water to a boil. Add the pasta, stir well, and cook until al dente, about 11 minutes. Drain, return to the pot, add the butter, and toss well to coat.

TO SERVE, divide the buttered tagliatelle among warmed plates and top with the vegetables. Snip the strings on the pork, carve into $\frac{1}{2}$-inch-thick slices, and place on top of the vegetables. Serve at once.

South : Apulia, Basilicata, Calabria, Campania

Apulia (called Puglia on Italian wine labels), the heel of Italy's boot, has been anonymous for so long that, if it were a person, it couldn't cash a check or get a restaurant reservation. To the prosperous northern Italians, Apulia is a shrug, a minor interruption. Yet, to the exasperation of the southerners, the rest of Italy eats the region's abundant vegetables and fruit, nibbles their smooth mozzarella, liberally pours their excellent olive oil, mops up its sauce with their bread (the best in Italy), and has always washed everything down with wines that were "corrected" by blending in the liquid sunshine of the south, all the while looking the other way and murmuring of other things.

Basilicata and Calabria are the arch and toe of the boot, Italy's poorest areas, isolated by topography (Basilicata is more than 90 percent mountainous, Calabria is bordered by mountains), punished by nature with floods and earthquakes. Basilicata has one great, if difficult, wine; Calabria has a few at least notable if rustic wines, but struggles with consistency. Neither will ever have the exuberance of Campania, their neighbor just to the north, which gave the world pizza, tomato sauce, stuffed eggplant, and a new outlook on garlic, thanks to the emigration of hundreds of thousands of Neapolitans.

For many centuries, southern Italy, and especially Apulia, was known as the country's wine cellar, producing huge amounts of wine that were shipped north, anonymously, to blend with and boost less vigorous wines. When Italy's wine renaissance began a few decades ago, the south was slow to join; many of the original band of winemaking pioneers who struggled along in the 1980s were outsiders. Still, the potential was always there—an abundance of sunshine especially, good soil, and distinctive native grapes—and it's now being realized so rapidly we old-timers can hardly keep up. Many of the wines are still somewhat rustic, and not at all elegant, but they're also delicious in vigorous, unassuming styles, wines to drink with pleasure, rather than to mull over.

Red Wines

Primitivo

Genetic research has proven what a lot of us suspected for a long time: the Primitivo of Apulia is in fact the ancestor of California's Zinfandel. The reason no one was totally sure was that the winemaking in the region was so rough and rustic that it was difficult to find a true benchmark Primitivo that showed more than a passing resemblance to Zinfandel. In the past ten years, well-financed vintners from northern Italy have moved in and invested in sophisticated vineyard techniques and modern winemaking technology. The result has been better grapes and better wines, with truer flavors. Now, spotting the similarities between Primitivo and Zinfandel is easy—and a pleasure.

The Primitivo vineyards aren't neat and tidy, as vineyards are in many places. In Apulia, the summer days are hot, and it's more efficient to let the vines grow bushy so the leaves protect the grapes from the sun. That heat does mean that the wines will be high in alcohol (as Zinfandel also usually is), fairly rich, softly tannic, and with an abundant fruitiness that comes across as slightly sweet. Also like Zinfandel, the wonderful fresh berry aromas seem to jump up out of the glass and fill a room.

Right now, the virtue of Primitivo is that, aside from being a lot cheaper, it's got many of Zinfandel's better qualities in a more relaxed and easygoing way. It has the exuberant fruitiness and likeability, without the ponderousness and oaky austerity of some Zins that strive for gold-medal status. It may be a younger sibling, but it's more fun to hang out with. Well-deserved international success has come quickly, and if ambitious winemakers don't mess it up by trying to make it into something big and serious, Primitivo will be one of any wine lover's best friends for a long time. (The name, incidentally, doesn't mean "primitive," even if that's what the wines were once. It is from a dialect word meaning "early riser," because it was the first grape to ripen every year, waking up early and quickly.)

TYPICAL AROMAS AND FLAVORS
Blackberries, cherries, plum jam, a hint of mint, spice, and perhaps licorice.

TIPS TO SUCCESSFUL MATCHES
WITH PRIMITIVO

- *Vigorous, sturdy, rustic food is lightened by Primitivo's soft amiability. Chunky pasta such as* orecchiette *tossed with sausages and green vegetables or cheesy tomato sauce, spicy lamb and potato casseroles, and char-grilled lamb chops are perfect matches. A wonderful cross-cultural match is Primitivo and a char-grilled cheeseburger (pecorino cheese, preferably).*

- *Few red wines succeed as well with hearty vegetable dishes, especially grilled vegetables. The zing of the acidity and softness of the tannin create a comfortable space for the flavors of mixed warm salads, stuffed eggplant, fried black olives, and even somewhat bitter greens such as arugula.*

Negroamaro

Here's a wine that got off to a bad start in international awareness, as it tended to live up to its name: "black, bitter." The grape has a tough skin that can make the wine rough and, yes, bitter, and certainly dark. The problem with old-fashioned winemaking was always a lack of full control once fermentation started. Sometimes, when the weather was warm, explosive fermentations resembled volcanic eruptions, with horribly predictable results. Now, with stainless-steel fermenting tanks that can be cooled down and regulated by computers, the wines have become tamer—and tastier. One Apulian winemaker told me he thought it could be the area's Pinot Noir, if only his fellow vintners had the sense to leave it alone, rather than to try and make it into a "big" wine.

It certainly has the same sort of lovely aroma, almost perfumed, that good Pinot Noir can have, and it has some hints of the same sort of nice black-cherry flavor, but the resemblance ends there. Negroamaro tends to be plumper and fuller, and the fruit doesn't have the same clear definition, but rather more of a mixed-berry summer-pudding aspect. It does finish up with a firm, dry astringency, however—a snap that brings you back for more.

Nomenclature still plays a part in its destiny. Given the dubious reputation of the wines that first came on the market, winemakers often prefer to call their Negroamaro simply *rosso*—"red"—with the name of an area attached; a further complication is that some blending is allowed. Thus, a wine might be 85 percent Negroamaro, which would qualify it as a varietal wine, but be labeled something like Rosso di Salento. As the variety has grown popular, the name's been creeping onto labels in small type, or noted on a back label, so it's always worth a look. You really shouldn't miss it.

Salice Salentino

This is very much the precursor wine to straight-ahead Negroamaro, named for the best-known of Apulia's wine regions, and another beneficiary of modern winemaking methods. It's a blend of Negroamaro and a small amount of Malvasia Nera. Malvasia is one of the oldest families of grapes, brought to Italy by the ancient Greeks. Most of the varieties in this extended family are white, wildly perfumed, and spicy, used to make sweet wines, but this is the one red exception. Even when made into a dry wine, it's still aromatic and a little spicy, so it adds a rich, almost flamboyant touch to Negroamaro: a small but intriguing, mysterious note in the aroma and flavor of the wine, unobtrusive but definitely there, and very nice, too.

TYPICAL AROMAS AND FLAVORS
Mixed berries, raisins, hints of cinnamon and Asian spices, a slight note of leather, and some earthiness in the aftertaste.

TIPS TO SUCCESSFUL MATCHES
WITH NEGROAMARO AND SALICE SALENTINO
- *Meat shouldn't be too strongly flavored, nor too meek. Both wines are fine with dark-meat poultry such as roast duck or guinea fowl, or grilled quail, turkey thighs, or pheasant. They are also very good with grilled tuna.*
- *Abundant fruit and aroma make the pair good partners for spicy and somewhat hot foods, including western Sicilian, Moroccan, Mexican, and Thai.*

Taurasi/Aglianico

Taurasi is a zone in Campania, east of Naples, and the wine of the same name is made from the Aglianico grape. For a long time, the regional name was better known than the grape because one family winery, Mastroberadino, made terrific wine there. Now, new winemakers have moved into neighboring areas of Campania, and into the next region, Basilicata, and they usually use the name of the grape, raising its profile enormously (though in Basilicata, it's perhaps unfortunately known as Aglianico del Vulture, after Mount Vulture, the extinct volcano where the vineyards are planted).

By whatever name, Aglianico is not a wine to take lightly. It's tannic and dense, and though its fruit is lovely, it often remains in the background of the flavor. It is not an easy wine, at least not when it's young—like any adolescent, really, just bigger and stronger. Aglianico's saving grace is that its promise is all up-front, and genuine. It may be dense, but it's not harsh, just multilayered in soft tannins. Eight or ten years after the vintage, the color lightens from deep ruby to garnet, the slightly funky smells of tobacco and leather fade away, and the rich berry fruit steps forward and takes charge. It's not surprising that these are cult wines, prized by collectors with wine cellars. They're fascinating, difficult, and worth the effort.

TYPICAL AROMAS AND FLAVORS
Blackberry jam, plums, and cherries, densely packed together, with overtones of violets, mushrooms, tobacco, leather, and tar.

TIPS TO SUCCESSFUL MATCHES
WITH TAURASI/AGLIANICO

- *If the wine is less than eight years old, meet it head-on with flavor: grilled steak or thick lamb chops rubbed with garlic, sausages, pasta with rich tomato-based sauce and lots of herbs, or barbecued pork.*
- *If the wine is more than eight years old, and preferably ten, treat it with a little more respect, as a partner: filet mignon, beef stew, roast leg of lamb, roast pork, grilled calf's liver, even a bit of blue cheese.*

White Wines

Greco di Tufo

This is a rather literal name. The grape was brought by the Greeks, who conquered and then cultivated southern Italy, and the soil is *tufa*, porous volcanic rock that also gives its name to the central small town in Campania where it grows. It may be an antique grape, but the wine has a thoroughly contemporary, though subtle character. It tastes clearly of fruit, without any one type standing out, like a well-mixed fruit salad, with a nice follow-up of tartness and a hint of almonds in the aftertaste. Its lightness of flavor contrasts with its medium body, setting up a nice surprise when its taste hangs around longer than you first expect. It's casual without being too informal, restrained and just a little bit elegant, making it a perfect wine for easy drinking, with appetizers, or lunch.

TYPICAL FLAVORS AND AROMAS
Grapes, apples, lemon flowers, and a slight mineral note in the aftertaste.

TIPS FOR SUCCESSFUL MATCHES
WITH GRECO DI TUFO
- *Keep it simple: pasta with a sauce of fresh vegetables or of chopped tomato and herbs; roast chicken, salad of mozzarella, tomatoes, and basil; and soft, light cheeses.*
- *Don't overchill the wine—no more than an hour in the fridge, half an hour in ice—as the subtle edges of flavor and charm may be lost.*

Fiano di Avellino

One of Italy's most alluring wines, Fiano doesn't quite smell or taste like any other white wine from anywhere. Behind a fresh and lingering crisp-apple fruit flavor, there's a hint of herbs, especially a resin note reminiscent of basil, and an echo of hazelnuts in the aftertaste. As with Greco, it's an ancient grape, a favorite of the Romans. The hills of Campania don't look hospitable to any sort of agriculture, but Fiano thrives in the foggy coolness of the slopes.

There are basically two styles of Fiano. One is what might be called the standard style, and it's quite good indeed; in fact, many people prefer its relative subtlety and finesse. The other style leans toward bigness, either from late harvesting when the grapes are almost over-ripe, or from using partly dried grapes for the same effect, and some use of oak barrels to boost the short-term maturity. So far, this style is attractive, with the lightly complex natural character of the grape coming through. If overambition doesn't get in the way, it will remain an intriguing, delicious alternative.

TYPICAL AROMAS AND FLAVORS
Apples, pears, pineapple, hints of vanilla, herbs, toast; slightly earthy aftertaste.

TIPS TO SUCCESSFUL MATCHES
WITH FIANO DI AVELLINO
- *The wine has enough character to be one of those whites that can go with what are often thought of as red-wine dishes: baked stuffed eggplant, mushroom pizza, pork and tomato sauce for pasta, rolled veal birds.*
- *The herbal hint makes Fiano di Avellino a perfect match for fish cooked with herbs, such as sea bass stuffed with oregano, rockfish marinated with basil, or halibut baked in an envelope with mixed herbs.*

South **: Recipes**

Mushrooms Stuffed with Goat Cheese and Pesto

RECOMMENDED WINE: Fiano di Avellino

ALTERNATIVE WINE: Greco di Tufo

Goat cheese and basil have a tangy affinity for each other, and those flavors get a boost from anything savory, as in this dish, an excellent first course or light lunch.

¼ cup olive oil

1 clove garlic, peeled but left whole

salt and freshly ground black pepper

½ cup pine nuts

4 fresh portobello mushrooms

½ cup Pesto (page 196)

8 ounces fresh goat cheese, cut into
    ½-inch-thick slices, at room temperature

3 ounces arugula, tough stems removed

extra-virgin olive oil for dressing

SERVES 4

IN A SMALL SAUCEPAN, heat the olive oil over medium heat. Add the garlic, remove from the heat, season with salt and pepper, and let stand for 1 hour. Remove the garlic and discard.

IN A SMALL, DRY SKILLET, toast the pine nuts over medium-high heat, shaking the pan often. Remove from heat just as they begin to brown, after only a few minutes. They'll continue to cook off the heat. Pour into a small bowl.

PREHEAT THE BROILER. Line a broiler pan with aluminum foil.

REMOVE THE STEMS FROM THE MUSHROOMS AND DISCARD. Brush the tops of the mushrooms with the garlic-flavored oil and place, gill side down, on the prepared pan. Place in the broiler about 4 inches from the heat source and broil until lightly browned, about 10 minutes. Remove from the broiler and place the caps, gill side up, on a work surface. Set the broiler pan aside.

SPREAD THE PESTO ON THE GILL SIDE OF EACH MUSHROOM, dividing it equally. Place a slice of goat cheese in the center of each mushroom and return the mushrooms to the broiler pan. Broil until the cheese browns slightly, 2 to 3 minutes. Remove from the broiler and scatter the pine nuts around the cheese.

IN A BOWL, toss the arugula with just enough extra-virgin olive oil to dress the leaves lightly, then season with salt and pepper. Arrange a mound of arugula on each plate. Place a mushroom alongside and serve at once.

Francis Ford Coppola's
Fusilli alla Pappone

RECOMMENDED WINE: **Fiano d'Avellino**
ALTERNATIVE WINE: **Greco di Tufo**

Francis Ford Coppola is not only a great movie director, but also a serious vintner, owner of a historically important vineyard and winery in the Napa Valley, now known as Niebaum-Coppola. When it comes to winemaking, he calls himself "an amateur with my heart in the right place," but when it comes to cooking, he's very much hands-on. He started cooking for friends in college ("I didn't have much money, and it created a semblance of family away from home," he told me); perhaps that's why he named this dish for "gluttony." In college, it served four hungry students. At my house, it does well for six.

½ cup sunflower oil

1 pound zucchini, cut crosswise
　　into ⅛-inch-thick slices

1 pound fusilli

3 tablespoons unsalted butter

3 tablespoons olive oil

1 teaspoon all-purpose flour dissolved
　　in ⅓ cup milk

⅔ cup chopped fresh basil

¼ teaspoon salt

1 large egg yolk, lightly beaten

½ cup grated Parmesan cheese

¼ cup grated *pecorino romano* cheese

SERVES 6 AS A MAIN COURSE

IN A SKILLET, heat the sunflower oil over medium-high heat. In batches, add the zucchini and sauté until lightly browned on both sides, about 2 minutes on each side. With a slotted spoon, remove to paper towels to drain.

BRING A LARGE POT FILLED WITH SALTED WATER TO A BOIL. Add the pasta, stir well, and cook until al dente, about 12 minutes.

MEANWHILE, in a large skillet or heavy-bottomed saucepan, melt 1 ½ tablespoons of the butter with the olive oil over medium heat. When the butter foams, reduce the heat to low and slowly stir in the dissolved flour. Cook, stirring constantly, until the mixture begins to thicken, about 30 seconds. Add the zucchini and stir several times. Add the basil and salt and cook briefly, stirring, only until heated through. Remove from the heat and stir in the remaining 1 ½ tablespoons butter. Briskly stir in the egg yolk, then stir in the Parmesan and *pecorino romano* cheeses, mixing well.

DRAIN THE PASTA AND TRANSFER TO A LARGE WARMED BOWL. Add the sauce, toss thoroughly, and serve immediately.

Grilled Fish Steaks
on *Peperonata*

RECOMMENDED WINE: **Negroamaro**
ALTERNATIVE WINE: **Salice Salentino**

Peperonata is one of those wonderfully flexible Italian ideas, at once simple, definite, and elusive. Basically, it's a stew made from bell peppers and other vegetables, including onions and tomatoes, with additions according to what else grows in the region, the cook's whimsy, what else is on the table, and what grandma made when the cook was young (the standard version follows). This version is more abundant but not so pungent, because it's a supporting player to the fish.

1 tablespoon sea salt

2 tablespoons chopped fresh thyme

1 tablespoon fresh lemon juice

3 tablespoons olive oil

4 fish steaks such as swordfish or halibut with skin
   intact, each about 6 ounces and 1 inch thick

PEPERONATA:

5 tablespoons olive oil

2 olive oil–packed anchovy fillets,
   drained and chopped

1 clove garlic, chopped

1 onion, chopped

1 red bell pepper, seeded, deribbed,
   and cut into 1-inch pieces

1 yellow bell pepper, seeded, deribbed, and
   cut into 1-inch pieces

1 small eggplant, about 8 ounces,
   cut into 1-inch pieces

1 cup Tomato Essence (page 198)

½ cup cut-up green beans (1-inch lengths)

½ cup sliced zucchini (¼-inch-thick slices)

2 tablespoons capers, drained

2 tablespoons finely chopped fresh chives

SERVES 4

IN A MORTAR, combine the salt, thyme, lemon juice, and olive oil and grind together with a pestle. (Alternatively, mix together in a small bowl with the back of a spoon.) Spread the mixture over both sides of each fish steak, place on a platter, cover, and refrigerate for at least 1 hour or up to 3 hours. Remove from the refrigerator 30 minutes before cooking.

TO MAKE THE *PEPERONATA,* in a large heavy-bottomed saucepan, heat 2 tablespoons of the olive oil over medium heat. Add the anchovy, garlic, and onion, stir well, and cook, stirring, until the onion begins to color, 3 to 4 minutes. Add the remaining 3 tablespoons olive oil, the bell peppers, and the eggplant and cook, stirring often, for 15 minutes. Add the Tomato Essence, cover, and cook for 30 minutes. Add the green beans, zucchini, and capers, stir well, and reduce the heat to low. Re-cover and cook for 15 minutes more.

WHILE THE VEGETABLES ARE COOKING, light a fire in a charcoal grill, or preheat the broiler.

DURING THE LAST 15 MINUTES THE VEGETABLES ARE COOKING, the coals or the broiler should be ready. Pat the fish dry with paper towels. Place the fish on the well-oiled grill rack or on a broiler pan lined with aluminum foil. Grill or broil 4 to 6 inches from the heat source, turning once, until opaque and firm to the touch, about 5 minutes on each side.

TO SERVE, place a liberal helping of *peperonata* on each warmed plate and place a fish steak on top. Scatter the chives over all.

Warm Salad of **Squid** and **Vegetables**

RECOMMENDED WINE: **Fiano di Avellino**
ALTERNATIVE WINE: **Greco di Tufo**

There are only two ways to cook squid—very quickly or very slowly. Anything in-between, and it's like chewing delicious rubber bands. Along the shore in southern Italian beach resorts, there is usually at least one stand selling grilled fish, octopus, cuttlefish, and squid, which are either eaten on the spot or taken home and tossed into a salad. This is a slightly more elaborate version of that result.

2 pounds cleaned squid

½ cup, plus 2 tablespoons olive oil,
  plus extra for brushing

¼ cup, plus 2 teaspoons fresh lemon juice

2 cloves garlic, chopped

3 small globe eggplants, about 8 ounces each

2 red bell peppers, quartered lengthwise,
  seeded, and deribbed

4 Roma (plum) tomatoes, quartered lengthwise

2 medium zucchini, each cut on the diagonal
  into 6 slices

salt and freshly ground black pepper

24 fresh basil leaves

1 red Thai chili, seeded and minced

SERVES 4

PICK OVER THE SQUID, making sure there are no bits of bone at the base of the tentacles or strips of cartilage in the bodies. Slice the bodies into rings; leave the tentacles whole. Place the squid in a large, heavy-duty plastic bag. In a small bowl, whisk together ¼ cup of the olive oil, the ¼ cup lemon juice, and the garlic, and add to the bag. Seal the bag and shake well to coat the squid. Refrigerate for at least 2 hours or up to 3 hours. Remove from the refrigerator 30 minutes before cooking.

LIGHT A FIRE IN A CHARCOAL GRILL, or preheat the broiler.

CUT 1 EGGPLANT INTO QUARTERS LENGTHWISE, then cut crosswise into ½-inch-thick pieces. Cut the bell pepper quarters crosswise into ½-inch pieces. In a large bowl, combine the cut eggplant, the bell peppers, tomatoes, and zucchini. Add ¼ cup of the olive oil and season with salt and pepper. Toss to coat. Set aside to marinate.

continued

CUT THE REMAINING 2 EGGPLANTS IN HALF LENGTHWISE AND BRUSH THE CUT SIDES WITH OLIVE OIL. When the coals are hot (usually after about 30 minutes, when they're barely covered with gray ash and you can hold your hand about 4 inches above them for only 2 or 3 seconds) or the broiler is ready, place the eggplants, cut side up, on the grill rack 4 inches from the coals, or place them, cut side down, on a baking sheet covered with aluminum foil and slip into the broiler 4 inches from the heat source. Grill or broil until the skin is charred and the flesh is softened and cooked, about 20 minutes. Remove from the grill or broiler, let cool, and scoop the flesh out of the skin. Discard the skin.

IN A BLENDER OR FOOD PROCESSOR, combine the eggplant flesh with 1 tablespoon of the olive oil, 12 of the basil leaves, the chili, and a little salt. Process until smooth. Transfer to a bowl and stir in 1 teaspoon of the lemon juice to preserve the color. Set aside.

REMOVE THE SQUID FROM THE PLASTIC BAG AND DRAIN OFF ANY EXCESS MARINADE. Discard the marinade.

REMOVE THE VEGETABLES FROM THE MARINADE AND DISCARD THE MARINADE. Arrange the vegetables in a single layer in a hinged grill basket and cook over the coals, turning once, until lightly charred, about 4 minutes on each side. Or spread the vegetables in a single layer on the broiler pan lined with fresh aluminum foil and broil, turning once, about 4 minutes on each side. Transfer the vegetables to a platter. Mix together the remaining 1 tablespoon olive oil and 1 teaspoon lemon juice, and tear the remaining 12 basil leaves into pieces. Sprinkle both over the vegetables.

PLACE THE SQUID IN THE GRILL BASKET. Try to keep the tentacles, which scorch easily, amid the rings. Grill for no more than 2 minutes on each side over the coals. The squid turn brilliant white and opaque when done. Or spread the squid in a single layer on the broiler pan lined with fresh aluminum foil and broil, turning once, about 2 minutes per side.

SPREAD THE EGGPLANT PURÉE ONTO PLATES, arrange the grilled vegetables on top, and pile the squid on top of them. Serve warm.

Peperonata, with Variations

RECOMMENDED WHITES: Fiano di Avellino, Greco di Tufo
RECOMMENDED REDS: Negroamaro, Salice Salentino

This is the basic *peperonata,* in contrast to the more elaborate version that accompanies the fish steaks on page 149. Delicious and useful in many ways, it can be eaten hot, warm, or cold, as a topping for a slice of garlic toast, mixed with or alongside light meat or fish, or on its own as part of a buffet. Some versions include a dollop of wine vinegar; others call for celery or a lot of onion. But I think those additions detract from the vibrant sweetness of the peppers, as well as make the dish less wine friendly. I've included two variations, which complement the basic character of the dish. It will keep, covered and refrigerated, for up to a week, so it's also a good make-ahead dish. In any incarnation, this isn't a dish for heavy or tannic wines. Whether your preference is for white or red, the wine should be fresh and fruity.

⅓ cup olive oil

1 small onion, chopped

1 clove garlic, chopped

1 ½ pounds red bell peppers, seeded, deribbed, and cut lengthwise into ½-inch-wide strips

12 ounces tomatoes, peeled, seeded, and chopped

6 large fresh basil leaves, torn in half

salt

1 tablespoon chopped fresh parsley

SERVES 4

IN A LARGE HEAVY-BOTTOMED SAUCEPAN, heat the olive oil over medium-low heat. Add the onion and garlic and cook, stirring, until soft, about 10 minutes. Add the bell peppers, raise the heat to medium, and sauté just until they begin to brown, 10 to 15 minutes. Add the tomatoes, basil, and salt to taste and stir well. Add a few tablespoons warm water if the mixture seems dry. Cover, reduce the heat to medium-low, and cook until quite soft, about 20 minutes. Remove from the heat, stir in the parsley, and serve hot, warm, or at room temperature.

VARIATIONS:

- *Stir in 1 tablespoon balsamic vinegar at the end of cooking. This is a good variation if the dish will be served cool or cold.*
- *Cook 4 sausages in a skillet over medium heat until well browned and cooked through, about 15 minutes. Remove from the pan, cut into 1-inch chunks, and add with the tomatoes.*

Roasted Cod Fillets
with Tomato-Tapenade Crust

RECOMMENDED WINE: **Fiano diAvellino**
ALTERNATIVE WINE: **Greco di Tufo**

If you happen to have my Tomato Essence (page 198) and Olive Marmalade (page 200) in the fridge, the easy way to make the tapenade would be to combine them with a few capers, anchovies, and some basil and blend. If not, here's a simple version from scratch, using black olives. This recipe also works with fillets of any white fish, such as haddock, halibut, or even sea bass, if you can get them thick enough (more than 1 inch). The wine should be crisp and dry, fairly sturdy, and not too aromatic or fruity and light.

1 bunch fresh basil (at least 18 leaves), chopped

1/3 cup chopped, pitted black olives

3 olive oil–packed anchovy fillets, rinsed

1 tablespoon capers, rinsed

3 tablespoons Tomato Essence (page 198), or

    12 sun-dried tomatoes in oil, drained and chopped

2 cloves garlic, 1 chopped and 1 halved

1/4 cup, plus 2 tablespoons olive oil

1/4 cup fresh white bread crumbs, moistened

    with water

1 tablespoon fresh lemon juice

4 cod fillets, each about 8 ounces and

    1 inch thick, skinned

SERVES 4

PREHEAT THE OVEN TO 425°F.

IN A BLENDER, combine the basil, olives, anchovies, capers, Tomato Essence, and the chopped garlic, and process on high speed until smooth, 2 to 3 minutes. Adjust the speed setting to low, add 1/4 cup of the olive oil and the bread crumbs and process for another minute. It should be a slightly rough paste. Remove to a small bowl.

IN A SMALL SAUCEPAN, combine the remaining 2 tablespoons olive oil, the lemon juice, and the halved garlic clove over low heat and cook until the garlic releases its aroma and flavors the oil, about 5 minutes. Discard the garlic and pour some of the oil mixture into a roasting pan to coat the bottom. Put the cod fillets in the roasting pan, and pour the remaining oil mixture over them. Spoon the tapenade thickly over the top of each fillet.

ROAST THE FISH UNTIL THE FILLETS ARE FIRM TO THE TOUCH AND FLAKE EASILY, 10 to 12 minutes. Serve immediately.

Slow-Baked **Lamb** with Potatoes

RECOMMENDED WINE: **Primitivo**
ALTERNATIVE WINE: **Negroamaro**

In Apulia, many meals open with several small courses of delicious combinations of vegetables, followed by a simple meat dish, usually lamb. It's the cuisine of farmers in a region of agricultural abundance, but little ready cash. (Contemporary cooks have refined the table, and if I were condemned to a life of vegetarianism, I'd head for Apulia to live out my days.) This recipe is from my friend Susanna Gelmetti, who teaches cookery there.

1 cup fresh bread crumbs

1/2 cup grated Parmesan cheese

2 cloves garlic, chopped

1/4 cup chopped fresh parsley

2 tablespoons chopped fresh rosemary

2 tablespoons chopped fresh oregano

1 teaspoon freshly ground black pepper

3/4 cup olive oil

2 pounds waxy potatoes, peeled and
   cut into 1-inch chunks

salt

2 pounds boneless lean lamb shoulder or
   other lean cut, cut into 1-inch chunks

2 cups coarsely chopped, peeled tomatoes

3/4 cup dry white wine

SERVES 4

PREHEAT THE OVEN TO 400°F.

IN A BOWL, combine the bread crumbs, Parmesan, garlic, parsley, rosemary, oregano, and pepper and mix well. Pour 3 tablespoons of the olive oil into a Dutch oven or other heavy pot, to cover the bottom. Add a layer of potatoes, sprinkle lightly with salt, and spread a layer of the herb mixture evenly over the top. Add a layer of lamb, and spread all the tomatoes on top. Repeat the layers with the remaining potatoes, herb mixture, and lamb. Drizzle the wine and the remaining 1/2 cup olive oil over the top. Pour in enough water to cover the tomato layer (about 1 cup).

COVER THE POT, place in the oven, and cook for 45 minutes. Uncover and check the level of the liquid; the bottom layer should still be quite moist. If not, add 1/2 cup water. Return the pot, uncovered, to the oven and cook until a light crust has formed and the potatoes are tender, about 30 minutes longer. Serve at once.

Sweet-and-Sour Grilled Pork with Sage-Apple Stuffing

RECOMMENDED WINE: **Salice Salentino**
ALTERNATIVE WINE: **Aglianico del Vulture**

Sweet-and-sour combinations, known as *agrodolce* in Italian, are found all along the Mediterranean, probably a legacy of Arab traders (and sometimes conquerors). At the shore, balsamic vinegar is often used for subtle fish sauces, but inland, where *agrodolce* sauces are popular with game, the flavors are more typically robust. Here, the sweet-and-sour seasoning is integrated into the other flavors, enhancing the slow-cooked pork. The best wine match is a full-flavored red.

1 pound ground pork

2 tart apples such as Granny Smith, cored, peeled, and chopped

1 clove garlic, chopped

1 shallot, chopped

2 tablespoons chopped fresh sage

1/2 cup toasted dried bread crumbs

salt and freshly ground black pepper

2 tablespoons olive oil

1/4 cup honey

1/4 cup red wine vinegar

1 boneless pork shoulder roast (Boston butt), 5 to 6 pounds

SERVES 8 TO 10

IN A BOWL, combine the ground pork, apples, garlic, shallot, sage, bread crumbs, and a little salt and pepper and mix well. In a skillet, heat the olive oil over medium heat. Add the pork-apple mixture and cook, stirring, until the meat is cooked, 7 to 8 minutes. Remove from the heat and let cool.

LIGHT A FIRE IN A CHARCOAL GRILL WITH A COVER, using about 40 briquettes.

IN A SMALL SAUCEPAN, melt the honey in the vinegar over medium-low heat. Remove from the heat and let cool slightly.

PLACE THE PORK SHOULDER ON THE CUTTING BOARD. Butterfly it by slicing it horizontally nearly all the way through. Open it out, fat side down, and lightly pound it flat. Brush half the honey-vinegar mix over the cut surface. Spoon the pork-apple mixture on top of the pork. Working from the edge closest to you, roll up gently and tie with kitchen string at 2-inch intervals. Place 2 sheets of aluminum foil in a cross pattern on the work surface and place the pork in the center. Bring the foil up around the sides and over the top, crimping it slightly but not sealing it closed. Pour the remainder of the honey-vinegar mix around the edges of the open space at the top, so it runs down the outside of the meat.

WHEN THE COALS ARE HOT (usually after about 30 minutes, when they're barely covered with gray ash and you can hold your hand about 4 inches above them for only 2 or 3 seconds), move them to either side of the grate and place a metal drip pan between the two banks. A disposable aluminum roasting pan is a good choice. Place the wrapped pork on the grill rack, centering it over the drip pan, cover, and cook for 1 hour. Uncover, add 7 or 8 briquettes to each bank of coals, re-cover, and cook for another hour. Uncover, peel the foil away now (you may leave it on the grill, underneath the meat), add 7 or 8 more briquettes to each bank of coals, cover, and cook for a final hour. At this point, the pork will be very dark brown and very tender.

REMOVE THE PORK TO A PLATTER, cover loosely with aluminum foil, and let rest for 15 minutes. To serve, snip the strings and carve the pork into thick slices. Serve at once.

Islands : Sicily, Sardinia, Lipari, Pantelleria

Walking around the vegetable market near the Rialto Bridge in Venice any morning early in April, wearing an overcoat to hold off the chill, you'll be surprised to see ripe, bright red tomatoes. They are Italian tomatoes, too, not something shipped in half-green from the Southern Hemisphere, but instead vine-ripened, juicy beauties from Sicily, where the sun comes early and tends to linger.

So did everyone else, going back thousands of years: Greeks, Romans, Arabs, Normans when France was a collection of tribal strongholds, Germans, the British, the French again, and other Italian kingdoms. The Sicilians assimilated what they brought in, stirred it some more, and made a cuisine out of it as baroque as their architecture. The Arabs probably taught the Sicilians how to make pasta and certainly to use an array of spices, and they got them started on the road to ice cream, which they introduced to France in the seventeenth century. (Rich Sicilian gelato is still considered Italy's best ice cream.)

These days, many people in the wine business call Sicily the California of Italy, for a few reasons. One, of course, is the sunshine, and another is that a lot of the wine is varietal; that is, named after the principal grape, rather than geography. But the main reason is that Sicily is bustling and wide open to new ideas. For many generations, the wines were anonymous, robust wines made by cooperatives for blending elsewhere, either northern Italy or even France, but about ten years ago, the scene exploded. Many of the co-ops went broke, new money brought in new technology and modern methods, and

the younger generation of grape growers decided to go further than their parents, to replant their vineyards and then also make their own kind of wine from their own grapes (which, in many cases, were the international classics, like Chardonnay, Cabernet Sauvignon, Merlot, and especially Syrah). The rate of change has been dizzying, and quite exciting—good news for wine lovers.

The extensive new planting of vineyards devoted to well-known international grape varieties has meant that the new generation of Sicilian wines hit the ground running in international markets. We like best that to which we're accustomed, and both the grape names and the styles were familiar and comfortable. Sunshine says it all: Chardonnay in Sicily is a big, tropical-fruit bomb; Cabernet Sauvignon and Merlot are expansive and often braced with oak. None of them matches especially well anything but the boldest Italian, let alone specifically Sicilian, food. Only Syrah seems to have escaped the repetitive, uniform, international sort of blockbuster-wine cliché and taken on an Italian style.

Sardinia is another story of invasion and poverty, with an even more stark contrast between the wealthy vacationers on the beaches of the northern coast, known as the Costa Smeralda, and the locals inland, where it's as barren as it is beautiful. When invaders came, the natives melted back into the mountains; after a while, they stayed. The cooking is rustic, to say the least, but delivers full and vivid flavors. Sardinia was once ruled by Spain, which may account for the fact that its best-known red wine is based on a Spanish grape.

There is another notable category of Sicilian wines: sweet wines, unique and fascinating. Marsala, tasting of caramel and vanilla, and aged in wood casks, is made on the western side of Sicily, while Lipari and Pantelleria, two tiny islands nearby, provide lightly spicy, intensely fruity beauties, the former from the Malvasia grape, the latter from a type of Muscat. All are superb alone after dinner, or with desserts.

Red Wines

Nero d'Avola

Perhaps the best news from Sicily so far is Nero d'Avola, a really lovely wine, engaging and cheerful, quite lively. Its color is vibrant ruby, its aroma almost perfumed, its cherry fruitiness quite generous, and there's enough tannic firmness to suggest that it has the potential to age gracefully, at least for two or three years after the vintage (though it's pretty darn good at one year old, too). In the nondescript bad old days, the wine was valued for brightening up blends with other wines, so when the new era began, it was the prime candidate for stardom, and would have been an even bigger hit if there had been enough of it; new vineyard plantings will remedy that problem soon. No one knows where it originally came from, but its considerable charm means it's here to stay.

At the moment, two styles of Nero d'Avola are available: the fresh, sprightly, immediately likeable version, which is bursting with the fruity varietal character of the grape, and prominently labeled with its name, and those versions blended with Cabernet, Merlot, Syrah, or combinations thereof, often made for strength and aged in oak barrels for seriousness. The former are typically inexpensive, often made from young vines and sent to market early. Snap them up— they should be good value as well as delicious. The serious ones, often bearing a geographic designation of Cerasuolo di Vittoria (an area in the southeastern corner of Sicily), will mention Nero d'Avola somewhere on the front or back label and be more expensive, though still often good value, and worth stashing away until they're two or three years old.

TYPICAL AROMAS AND FLAVORS
Black cherries, cherry jam, sometimes more intense, as in plums, with hints of violets, roses, and spice.

TIPS TO SUCCESSFUL MATCHES
WITH NERO D'AVOLA

- *The lighter, varietally named style strikes a good balance with lighter meats such as roast veal, grilled veal chops or scaloppine, or pan-roasted pork tenderloin.*
- *The more serious style, which becomes fairly succulent with a little age, fits hand in glove with smooth-textured meats, such as rare roast beef or lamb chops, or thick slices of grilled tuna.*

Syrah

Of all the international (that is, non-Italian) grape varieties, Syrah deserves a special mention, because its character seems to have changed nicely in Sicily. You could say it's almost on its way to going native. In fact, some Sicilian winemakers insist that Syrah and Nero d'Avola are related, even going so far as to claim that Syrah originated in Sicily, which is wishful thinking of a very high order. On the other hand, Syrah from Sicily has the same sort of lovely aroma and vibrant brightness of flavor, combined with a touch of spice, as the best Syrahs from elsewhere.

The wine scene in Sicily is a mad scramble these days. Two years ago, there was little unblended varietal Nero d'Avola and only one Syrah available, while now there are a dozen of the latter. Styles are still being created, so it's hard to pin down an exact flavor profile except to say that they have generally tasted good, bursting with fruit, in early samplings and are worth seeking out. If you see a Sicilian red labeled simply *"rosso,"* check the back label. It's liable to be a Syrah blend, sometimes with Nero d'Avola, which is a good parlay. Its aromas, flavors, and uses are similar to those of Nero d'Avola.

Cannonau

The flavor rings a distant bell, a memory of something, but hard to pin down. Spain? France? Australia? Actually, it's all of the above, for Cannonau is the name in Sardinia for Grenache, the second most widely planted grape variety in the world. It's a workhorse grape, strong enough to provide good dry rosé in Spain and Australia and lending backbone to blends in Rioja and France's Rhône Valley and Provence. On its own everywhere in the world, and especially in Sardinia, it can make a fairly fierce wine, highly alcoholic and robust. In fact, there's nothing subtle about it at all: it seems inevitably rustic, incapable of being polished up. Very little Cannonau is exported, though it does sometimes show up on wine lists of restaurants owned by Sardinians (who will usually admit that it tends to be *selvatico*—"wild," with a flavor that's an odd combination of leather, tobacco, and cherries). If you see it and have a chance to at least taste it, give it a try. You might go to Sardinia some day, and it would be good to be prepared.

White Wines

Inzolia

The white wines of Sicily made from native grapes don't amount to much in terms of distinct aromas and flavors. Inzolia is the best of the bunch. It has some fruity aromas and a middle-of-the-road, pleasant, lightly crisp flavor, but not much of a lingering aftertaste. There are numerous blends with small portions of Catarratto and Grecanico added, and they're a lot more interesting—the former adds body, the latter acidity, and both contribute a touch of complexity. Some versions list the variety on the front label; if you don't see it there, check the back label: several Sicilian whites are good examples. They'll still be in the easy-drinking category, but quite pleasant with food, too.

TYPICAL AROMAS AND FLAVORS
Melons, green apples, hint of elderflower.

TIPS TO SUCCESSFUL MATCHES
WITH INZOLIA

● *Simplest is best. The wine is a good, modest accompaniment to grilled fish or vegetable dishes, or even spicy pasta dishes.*

Catarratto

The most widely planted grape in Sicily, though not the most popular, is Catarratto, though not for table wine until recently. It's neutral, and so it has been used to make other kinds of wine, notably sweet Marsala and herbal Vermouth, and also has been blended in with other white grapes, mainly because its fullness provides body for other wines with more interesting aromas and acidity. Once in a while, it appears by itself, a triumph of hope over flavor, but it mostly shows up in varietally labeled blends (Catarratto and Chardonnay, Catarratto and Inzolia, and so on) that are invariably mass-market, undemanding warm-weather sippers.

Grecanico

The third junior partner in Sicilian blends, and occasionally pushed into the spotlight on its own, Grecanico is valued for its acidity. In good hands and in good years, it can be a nice, tight, crisp wine by itself, and can occasionally make the step up to matching food, especially spicy or tomato-based fish dishes, or a mixed grill of fish. Worth trying.

Vermentino

Vermentino is Italy's up-and-coming white grape, now being planted in several areas, but well established in Sardinia. No one knows where it came from, although it has put down roots for a couple of hundred years around the Mediterranean, in France as well as Italy. Sardinia, which is hot, with rocky soil, seems to suit the grape just fine, and as the winemaking has improved, so has the reputation of Vermentino, now being widely planted in Tuscany, too. It's medium bodied but feels bigger, almost expansive, and has a definite, but not sharp, acidity, with a fairly persistent aftertaste. The aroma and flavor both suggest a mixture of herbs, a sort of bouquet garni, quite intriguing, although the wine can tire out your palate when drunk on its own. On the other hand, it's a very good food wine, adaptable and amiable.

TYPICAL AROMAS AND FLAVORS
Apples, melons, lemon flowers, fennel, sage, sometimes a hint of resin.

TIPS TO SUCCESSFUL MATCHES
WITH VERMENTINO

- *Avoid food cooked with too many herbs, which might go head-to-head with the herbal top notes of the wine. Grilled pork or fish, or either in a stew with tomatoes, would complement the wine perfectly.*
- *Full-flavored seafood such as lobster, squid, and shrimp come into their own with the fullness of Vermentino, which also flatters their sweetness.*

Islands **: Recipes**

Swordfish Rolls

RECOMMENDED WINE: **Nero d'Avola**
ALTERNATIVE WINE: **Chardonnay**

Thin slices of swordfish rolled around various kinds of stuffing are a Sicilian specialty, and this recipe, from Messina, is one of the simplest but most delicious. The cheese, a staple in southern Italy, is available from good cheese shops. It's full flavored but mellow and just slightly tangy. If it's unavailable, substitute young provolone or pecorino. At the Tenuta di Donnafugata winery, guests are served this dish as part of a welcoming buffet, with red wine. If you prefer white wine, one of the new breed of Sicilian Chardonnays would be a good choice.

salt

1 small onion, finely chopped

1 can (14 ounces) Roma (plum) tomatoes, coarsely chopped, with juice

1/2 cup Gaeta or other flavorful black olives, pitted and halved

2 tablespoons capers, rinsed

1 small celery stalk, chopped, blanched in boiling water for 2 minutes, and drained

2 pounds swordfish, in one cross-section piece, about 3 inches thick

2/3 cup grated *caciocavallo* cheese

3 tablespoons chopped fresh basil leaves

3 tablespoons chopped fresh flat-leaf parsley

2 tablespoons fresh bread crumbs

5 tablespoons olive oil

freshly ground black pepper

SERVES 6 AS A FIRST COURSE

IN A LARGE HEAVY-BOTTOMED SAUCEPAN, combine a few tablespoons water and a sprinkling of salt and bring to a simmer. Add the onion and cook, uncovered, until the onion is translucent, about 5 minutes. Add the tomatoes and their juice, olives, capers, and celery, reduce the heat to medium-low, and cook until slightly reduced and the flavors have blended, about 15 minutes. Remove from the heat and set aside.

IF YOU CAN, ask your fishmonger to cut the fish into 12 thin slices, each 1/4 inch thick. If you aren't able to have your fish-monger slice the fish, here's the best way to do it: Place the piece of fish in the freezer for 15 minutes; this isn't enough to freeze it, but it will firm up and be easier to slice. Trim off and discard the skin. With a very sharp knife, cut the fish into 1/4-inch-thick slices. Trim each slice into a shape as close to a rectangle as possible, ideally 3 to 4 inches wide.

FINELY CHOP THE SWORDFISH TRIMMINGS, and place them in a bowl. Add the cheese, basil, parsley, bread crumbs, and olive oil and season with salt and pepper. Lay out the fish slices on a work surface and spread an equal amount of the mixture on each one. Roll up each slice from the short end and secure with toothpicks or tie with kitchen string.

RETURN THE SAUCEPAN WITH THE SAUCE TO MEDIUM HEAT, add the rolls, cover, and cook for 10 minutes. Uncover, turn the rolls over, and cook, uncovered, until the fish is opaque throughout and firm to the touch, 10 to 12 minutes more.

SERVE THE SWORDFISH ROLLS HOT OR AT ROOM TEMPERATURE, with the sauce spooned over the top.

Orange, Fennel, and Olive Salad with Mint

RECOMMENDED WINE: **Inzolia**

ALTERNATIVE WINE: **Grecanico**

Most Sicilian farms have an abundance of both oranges and olives. Fennel, wild or cultivated, is also likely to be growing. This salad, a summertime staple on the island, owes its existence to more than availability, however. It's also delicious and refreshing. The idea of adding mint, making it even more refreshing, was given to me by an Australian winemaker of Sicilian descent, so I guess it's still all in the family. Use the best-quality olive oil you can find in this salad. Organic fennel is more tender than the wild variety, and has the most flavor. The best way to slice it thinly is with a mandoline, or you might try the slicing blade on the side of a cheese grater. The best wine is white, crisp, and cold.

4 fennel bulbs

¼ cup extra-virgin olive oil

1 tablespoon fresh lemon juice

salt and freshly ground black pepper

4 navel oranges

½ cup fresh mint leaves, roughly chopped

1 cup Gaeta or other flavorful black olives, pitted

SERVES 8

TRIM THE FENNEL BULBS, cut in half lengthwise, and cut away the hard core at the base. Thinly slice crosswise. Place in a large bowl. In a small bowl, whisk together the olive oil and lemon juice. Drizzle over the fennel, toss to coat, and season with salt and pepper.

CUT A THIN SLICE OFF THE TOP AND BOTTOM OF EACH ORANGE, revealing the flesh. Cut away the peel and pith from the sides. Cut each orange in half through the stem end, and then cut crosswise into thin slices. Add the orange slices to the fennel along with the mint and toss well.

SERVE THE SALAD ON A CHILLED PLATTER, with the olives scattered over the top.

Grilled Skewered Fish
with Mixed Vegetables

RECOMMENDED WINE: **Vermentino**
ALTERNATIVE WINE: **Inzolia**

In rural areas in the south of Italy, vegetables often co-star with meat or fish, and even the more humble of them, like chickpeas, turn out to be more interesting in the sort of combinations that home cooks devise (or improvise, perhaps). One day, cleaning out the fridge and coming upon a bit of Tomato Essence and some Chickpea Sauce, I realized I had a chance to do the same sort of combining, and discovered a perfect full-flavored partner for meaty grilled fish, rustic but satisfying. A little buttered pasta is a good accompaniment, and the best wine match should be aromatic, with good crisp acidity.

MARINADE:

½ cup olive oil

2 tablespoons chopped fresh thyme

3 cloves garlic, minced

½ teaspoon freshly ground black pepper

1 pound halibut, tuna, or swordfish fillet
    cut into chunks 1 ½ inches long by 1 inch thick

12 shallots, cut in half

2 red bell peppers, seeded, deribbed,
    and cut into ½-inch chunks

2 pounds spinach, well rinsed and
    tough stems removed

2 tablespoons minced fresh chives

1 cup Tomato Essence (page 198)

1 cup Chickpea Sauce, Lucchese Style (page 197)

SERVES 4

TO MAKE THE MARINADE, in a large bowl, whisk together the olive oil, thyme, garlic, and pepper. Add the fish, shallots, and bell peppers, stirring gently to coat them with the marinade. Cover and refrigerate for between 3 and 4 hours. Remove the fish from the refrigerator 30 minutes before cooking.

LIGHT A FIRE IN A CHARCOAL GRILL, or preheat the broiler. Soak 4 long wooden skewers in water for 30 minutes.

THE VEGETABLES CAN BE HEATED IN A PREHEATED 350°F OVEN, if you are not using the broiler, or in a microwave. Put the spinach, with just the rinsing water clinging to the leaves, in a saucepan, cover, and cook just until wilted, about 2 minutes. Drain in a sieve, pressing out the excess water, set aside to cool slightly, and then chop finely. In a bowl, toss together the spinach, chives, Tomato Essence, and Chickpea Sauce. Transfer to a baking dish and heat for 20 minutes in the preheated oven, or for 2 minutes on full power in the microwave.

DRAIN THE SKEWERS. Remove the fish chunks from the marinade and thread them onto the skewers, alternating them with the shallot halves and bell pepper pieces. (This messy step is best done over a platter, with some paper towels handy.) Discard the marinade.

WHEN THE COALS ARE HOT (usually after about 30 minutes, when they're barely covered with gray ash and you can hold your hand about 4 inches above them for only 2 or 3 seconds) or the broiler is ready, place the skewers on the well-oiled grill rack or on a broiler pan lined with aluminum foil. Grill or broil 4 to 6 inches from the heat source, turning as necessary until the fish is just opaque throughout, about 10 minutes (it's better if the fish is slightly underdone, rather than overdone and dried out; test a chunk to see).

TO SERVE, spoon a bed of vegetables onto warmed plates and top with a skewer of fish.

Roast Stuffed Turkey
with Marsala Sauce

RECOMMENDED WINE: Nero d'Avola

ALTERNATIVE WINE: Syrah

One of the best turkey dishes I ever had was in the Piedmont, at one of my all-time favorite restaurants, Guido, in Costigliole d'Asti. I was on my honeymoon, but even so, I believe it was wonderful. It was also simplicity itself: thin slices of organic turkey breast lightly poached in spicy extra-virgin olive oil—as tender as can be imagined, served by themselves, and delicious. Since then, I've surprised myself by ordering turkey in several other Italian regions, as I can't resist seeing what this nation of ingenious cooks is going to do with it. Italians like turkey, and for holidays they cook up quite elaborate preparations, often boning the birds and stuffing them with rich combinations of fruits, nuts, and meats. Here's a simpler version that may at least provide a more interesting variation than the usual roast bird, with a bit of rich sauce for an extra kick. It also lends itself to any of several fruity, cheerful Italian reds. In fact, they're superb partners for most versions of turkey.

1 turkey, 10 to 12 pounds

salt

2 tablespoons olive oil, plus more
   for coating turkey

1 onion, finely chopped

4 cloves garlic, minced

1 pound ground pork

8 ounces sweet Italian sausages,
   removed from casings

2 cups loosely packed, cubed sourdough
   bread, without crusts

minced zest of 1 orange

1/4 cup fresh orange juice

1 tablespoon chopped fresh sage

1 tablespoon chopped fresh thyme

1 1/4 cups pitted prunes, cut into quarters

3 tablespoons hazelnuts, chopped

1/2 cup grated Parmesan cheese

1 cup dry Marsala *(fine)*

3 tablespoons minced fresh rosemary

3 ounces pancetta, finely chopped

freshly ground black pepper

1 cup reduced-sodium canned chicken broth

1 tablespoon unsalted butter,
   at room temperature

1 tablespoon all-purpose flour

SERVES 12

PREHEAT THE OVEN TO 350°F. Rinse and dry the turkey, then rub the inside with salt.

IN A MEDIUM-LARGE SKILLET, heat 1 tablespoon of the olive oil over medium heat. Add the onion and half the garlic and cook, stirring often, until soft, about 5 minutes. Add the pork and sausages and cook, stirring, until the meats lose their raw color, about 10 minutes. Remove from the heat and let cool.

MEANWHILE, in a large bowl, combine the bread cubes, orange zest and juice, sage, thyme, prunes, hazelnuts, Parmesan, and ½ cup of the Marsala and 1 tablespoon of the olive oil. Add the cooked meat and mix well. Set aside. In a small bowl, combine the rosemary, pancetta, and the remaining garlic and mix well. Beginning at the back of the bird, near the body cavity, loosen the skin of the turkey across the breast by inserting a finger under the skin and running it side to side and then forward. Insert the rosemary mixture under the skin and massage it so that it covers the breast meat fairly evenly. Stuff the body cavity with the bread mixture and skewer the cavity closed.

PLACE THE BIRD, breast side up, on a rack in a roasting pan. Brush or rub the skin liberally with olive oil, then rub with salt and pepper. Roast, basting every 30 minutes for the first 1½ hours with ½ cup Marsala and thereafter with the pan juices, until the juices run clear when the thigh joint is pricked, about 3 hours (figure on 18 minutes to the pound). Remove from the oven, cover loosely with aluminum foil, and let rest for 15 minutes.

WHILE THE TURKEY IS RESTING, make the sauce. Place the roasting pan over medium heat. Add the broth and bring the pan juices to a simmer, scraping up any browned bits from the bottom of the pan. Pour the juices into a bowl, let the fat rise to the top, and skim off with a spoon, or use a gravy separator. Pour the defatted juices into a small heavy-bottomed saucepan and bring to a simmer over medium heat. Mix together the butter and flour to form a paste. Gradually whisk the paste into the simmering liquid and continue to whisk until thickened; keep warm.

REMOVE THE SKEWERS FROM THE TURKEY AND SPOON THE STUFFING FROM THE CAVITY INTO A BOWL. Carve the turkey and arrange on a platter. Pour the sauce into a warmed serving bowl and pass at the table.

Sarah's **Guinea Hens** alla Rusticana

RECOMMENDED WINE: **Syrah**
ALTERNATIVE WINE: **Cannonau**

In Italian, the guinea hen was once called *gallina di faraona,* "hen of the pharoah," because it was originally imported from Egypt. Today, the name has been shortened to *faraona.* The meat is dark and slightly gamey, which gave my wife, a country girl and occasional hunter, the idea of creating this sauce. It is dense and deep and very slightly pungent, a delicious throwback to the direct flavors of game cookery. The recipe works as well with Cornish game hens, but you will need to shorten the cooking time by about 10 minutes. Serve the hens and their sauce over mashed or crushed potatoes. The wine needs to be savory, and certainly red.

> 1 ½ ounces dried porcini mushrooms
>
> 1 ½ cups boiling water
>
> 8 olive oil–packed anchovy fillets,
>   soaked in milk and drained
>
> 3 cloves garlic, chopped
>
> ¾ cup tomato paste
>
> ⅔ cup oil-packed black olives, pitted
>   and chopped
>
> 1 ½ cups dry red wine
>
> 1 ½ cups reduced-sodium canned chicken broth
>
> pinch of cayenne pepper
>
> salt and freshly ground black pepper
>
> 2 tablespoons sunflower oil
>
> 2 guinea hens, about 1 ¼ pounds each,
>   quartered
>
> ¼ cup sweet Marsala *dolce*

SERVES 4

PUT THE MUSHROOMS IN A SMALL HEATPROOF BOWL, pour the boiling water over them, and let soak for 30 minutes to soften. Drain the mushrooms, discarding the soaking liquid. Rinse under running cold water, chop roughly, and set aside.

IN A MORTAR, combine the anchovies and garlic and mash together with a pestle. (Alternatively, combine the ingredients in a bowl and mash with a fork.) In a bowl, combine the anchovy-garlic paste, mushrooms, tomato paste, olives, wine, broth, and cayenne pepper. Season with salt and pepper and mix well.

IN A HEAVY SKILLET, heat the sunflower oil over medium heat. Working in batches, brown the hen pieces on all sides. Place the sauce mixture in a Dutch oven or other heavy pot over medium heat and bring to a strong simmer. Add the browned hens. Reduce the heat to medium-low and return the liquid to a simmer. Cover and cook until the hens are tender, about 45 minutes.

USING A SLOTTED SPOON, remove the hens to a warmed plate and cover loosely with aluminum foil. Add the Marsala to the pot, stir well, and cook over medium heat until the aroma rises and the sauce takes on a silky sheen, about 2 minutes. Spoon the sauce over the hens to serve.

Grilled Tuna with Moroccan Spices

RECOMMENDED WINE: Nero d'Avola
ALTERNATIVE WINE: Chardonnay

Sicily is close to North Africa, and there's an overlap in and around Trapani, on the island's western shore, where immigrants haggle in the street markets and the food smells that hang on the air are heavy with spices like cumin, cinnamon, and cloves. The pasta of choice here is couscous, often combined with fish, black pepper, saffron, and cinnamon. In the multicultural context that prevails, that's Sicilian. This recipe creates the same sort of interplay of flavors, with the marinade forming a crisp, spicy coating as the fish cooks over the coals. It's full flavored enough to go well with red, but if it's a warm day or you prefer a white, Sicilian Chardonnay has the muscle to manage, too.

4 tuna steaks, each about 6 ounces
  and 1 inch thick

6 tablespoons chopped fresh cilantro

6 tablespoons chopped fresh parsley

¼ cup chopped green onions

2 cloves garlic, roughly chopped

1 teaspoon ground cumin

1 teaspoon ground coriander

1 teaspoon paprika

grated zest and juice of 1 lemon

4 tablespoons olive oil

SERVES 4

RINSE THE TUNA STEAKS AND PAT THEM DRY. Place them in a single layer in a small baking dish. In a blender or food processor, combine all the remaining ingredients and process until smooth. Pour the mixture over the fish, and turn the fish several times to coat thoroughly. Cover and refrigerate for about 2 hours, turning once to keep the fish moist. Remove the fish from the refrigerator 30 minutes before cooking.

LIGHT A FIRE IN A CHARCOAL GRILL, or preheat the broiler. When the coals are hot (usually after about 30 minutes, when they're barely covered with gray ash and you can hold your hand about 4 inches above them for only 2 or 3 seconds) or the broiler is ready, remove the fish from the marinade. Place on the well-oiled grill rack or on a broiler pan lined with aluminum foil. Grill or broil 4 to 6 inches from the heat source, turning once, until the tuna is browned on the outside (the marinade will sear into the tuna) but still medium-rare in the center, about 3 minutes on each side.

TRANSFER THE TUNA TO WARMED PLATES AND SERVE AT ONCE.

Desserts

Desserts in Italy tend to be reserved for special occasions, such as holidays or celebrations, or for a big night out at a restaurant. Otherwise, delicious but simple cakes or cookies suffice, or even fresh fruit and nuts. There is also little regionality with desserts: dishes like tiramisu, *panna cotta,* zabaglione, and *cassata* turn up everywhere, regardless of their origins. I've chosen a couple of classics and some of my own variations to complement and enhance the more notable dessert wines you might encounter—or seek out.

Dessert Wines

Marsala

Of all the rejuvenations, comebacks, reinventions, and transformations that various Italian wines have gone through in the past twenty years, none was so necessary or dramatic as that of Marsala—nor so overdue. It's a wine richer in history than most. In 1773, an English merchant sheltered his ship in Marsala's harbor, and he was so enthusiastic about the wine he discovered in the local taverns that he immediately sent a large consignment home to Liverpool, where it was also well received, and a thriving export business was born. (Marsala's patron saint is Saint Thomas of Canterbury, celebrated with a magnificent part-Corinthian-style cathedral.) Admiral Horatio Nelson was one of the first fans of the wine, calling it "a real luxury for our sailors." By the nineteenth century, Marsala was being exported around the world, and received the highest accolade of all, praise from the great French gourmet Anthelme Brillat-Savarin.

It's a fortified wine, averaging 17 to 19 percent alcohol, and made in several styles, ranging from fairly dry to very sweet. It's lovely to drink, but also magical to cook with, deepening and enriching sauces for all sorts of foods, from fish to poultry to meat and, of course, dessert. Therein lay its downfall, though. When sales slowed in the mid-twentieth century, Marsala was tinkered with. Premixed versions meant for rich sauces began to appear (concoctions of wine and egg cream, or coffee, for example), while the normal versions were heavily promoted merely as cooking wines. After a while, to be seen drinking the stuff was pretty much an admission that you were hopelessly unsophisticated. Being whipped into zabaglione or gravy became Marsala's typical fate.

In 1984, the winemakers decided to "relaunch an image of authenticity for this historical wine." They did so by restricting a number of additives and prohibiting the use of the term "Marsala" on bottles of the concocted products. (Several of them did not, however, stop making the concoctions, so possibilities for confusion still exist.) Only time will tell if it was a strategy that will prove to be too little too late.

By any measure, several proper Marsalas in various styles are lovely wines, and always worth trying. From a wide array of types—*fine, superiore, superiore riserva,* and *vergine/solera,* some *secco* (dry) and some *dolce* (sweet)—the most common, and very easy to like, are the dry or sweet wines in the middle: *superiore secco* is aged for at least two years and has a nutty, toffeelike character. It can be drunk as a rich aperitif or after dinner with an aged cheese. *Superiore dolce* is also aged for two years, but is unctuous and sweet, with caramel and dried-apricot overtones on top of its toffee character. It's wonderful with chocolate, or by itself after dinner as a contemplative pleasure.

Malvasia delle Lipari

Malvasia grapes, grown on the slopes of an extinct volcano on the tiny island of Lipari, north of Sicily, are spicy, giving the wine a unique, exotic aroma that jumps right out of the glass. It reeks of apricots, oranges, lemon flowers, and cinnamon—enthralling and unmistakable. The flavor is sweet, but that spice, and a good jolt of underlying acidity, is bracing. Serve it lightly chilled with fresh fruit like pears, or a simple apricot tart.

Moscato di Pantelleria

Sweet, spicy, and sexy, this wine is almost dessert in itself. The Muscat grapes are grown in a perennially hot zone on the small island of Pantelleria, south of Sicily. The characteristic muskiness of the semidried Muscats marries with aromas and flavors of honey, apricot, orange, cinnamon, golden raisins, and caramel in a rich, concentrated package. There's enough acidity still lurking in the background to make this a fairly serious wine, ideal with classic Sicilian desserts such as *cassata* or cannoli.

Chestnut-Infused *Panna Cotta* with Gingered Apricot Compote

RECOMMENDED WINE: **Marsala** *dolce*
ALTERNATIVE WINE: **Moscato di Pantelleria**

Originally from the Piedmont, *panna cotta* (cooked cream) is now made everywhere. I created this version when I got some chestnut purée for a completely different dish, and remembered the lovely rich flavor when I was planning a birthday dinner. The compote is a staple around our house, a good partner for ice cream, rice pudding, and even satisfying on its own.

PANNA COTTA:

1 envelope unflavored gelatin

¼ cup cold water

1 quart heavy cream

2 tablespoons chestnut purée (see note)

1 cup sugar

COMPOTE:

2 cups (12 ounces) dried apricots, finely chopped

3 tablespoons crystallized ginger (see note)

1 tablespoon honey

½ cup apple juice

SERVES 8

TO MAKE THE *PANNA COTTA*, in a small cup, sprinkle the gelatin over the water. Let soften for 5 minutes. Pour the cream into a heavy-bottomed saucepan, place over medium-low heat, and bring to a near simmer (the surface should just begin to move). Gently whisk in the softened gelatin, and then gently whisk in the chestnut purée. Finally, whisk in the sugar until it is fully dissolved, about 5 minutes. Do not let the mixture boil. Remove from the heat and let cool completely.

POUR THE COOLED MIXTURE INTO EIGHT ½-CUP RAMEKINS OR OTHER SMALL MOLDS. Cover and refrigerate for several hours until firm.

TO MAKE THE COMPOTE, in a heavy-bottomed saucepan, combine the apricots, ginger, and water just to cover. Place over medium heat and bring to a simmer. Stir well, reduce the heat to low, cover, and cook until the fruit begins to soften, about 20 minutes. Check occasionally to be sure there's enough liquid to prevent scorching. Remove from the heat, add the honey and apple juice, and stir well. Return to the heat, still at a low setting, and simmer gently, stirring occasionally, for another 30 minutes. At this point, the fruit will be extremely soft. Remove from the heat and let cool. (The compote can be made a few days in advance—in fact, it's better the second day—covered, and stored in the refrigerator. Bring to room temperature before serving.)

TO SERVE, spoon the compote onto flat plates and unmold a ramekin of *panna cotta* onto each one (for easier unmolding, dip the base of each ramekin in hot water for a moment before turning the *panna cotta* out onto the fruit). Serve at once.

NOTE: *The chestnut purée and crystallized ginger are usually stocked in the baking section of supermarkets. The chestnut purée typically comes in a tube, like toothpaste, and is sometimes lightly flavored with vanilla, which is a fine addition. The ginger is usually sold in small chunks in plastic tubs.*

Panettone **Raisin Custard**

RECOMMENDED WINE: **Marsala**
ALTERNATIVE WINE: **Moscato d'Asti**

Panettone, the slightly sweet, domed bread studded with bits of glazed fruit and raisins, originated in Milan. It is often baked using a "mother" yeast that may be decades old, which gives it a special, highly distinctive character—as light as air and rich and chewy at the same time. The breads have become so popular that Italian bakeries ship them, each loaf sealed in an airtight bag, around the world. My family makes a weekend of one, eating a few slices fresh on Saturday, toasting a couple of slices for breakfast Sunday, and finishing up with what's left baked into custard for dessert that night. For company, we make a large-scale custard and cut the pannetone the night before so that the slices dry out a bit, which provides the best texture. It's a perfectly delicious match with sweet, late-harvest wines.

$1/2$ cup golden raisins

1 panettone, about 1 pound

3 tablespoons unsalted butter,
    at room temperature

3 cups milk

2 cups heavy cream

pinch of salt

2 vanilla beans, split in half lengthwise

6 large eggs

1 cup granulated sugar

$1/2$ teaspoon ground cinnamon

$1/4$ cup superfine sugar

SERVES 8

IN A SMALL BOWL, soak the raisins in warm water to cover for 30 minutes to soften.

PREHEAT THE OVEN TO 375°F.

TRIM OFF THE ROUNDED SIDES OF THE PANETTONE TO MAKE THEM SQUARE, then cut the loaf into 1-inch-thick slices. Using a little of the butter, lightly butter the bottom of a square, flameproof 2-quart baking dish. Use the remaining butter to spread on one side of each panettone slice. Place the slices, slightly overlapping and buttered side up, neatly in the dish.

IN A HEAVY-BOTTOMED SAUCEPAN, combine the milk, cream, salt, and vanilla beans and heat over medium-low heat until bubbles begin to appear around the edge of the pan. Remove from the heat. In a large bowl, whisk together the eggs and granulated sugar until well blended. Slowly pour about $1/2$ cup of the hot milk mixture into the egg mixture while whisking. Then slowly whisk the egg mixture into the saucepan. Set aside.

SPRINKLE THE PANETTONE WITH THE CINNAMON. Drain the raisins and scatter them evenly across the slices. Carefully pour the milk mixture through a fine-mesh sieve held over the baking dish. Discard the vanilla beans.

BAKE THE CUSTARD UNTIL SET, about 45 minutes. Remove from the oven and set aside. Just before serving, preheat the broiler. Sprinkle the surface of the custard evenly with the superfine sugar. Place under the broiler 4 to 6 inches from the heat source for 1 to 2 minutes to create a brown glaze. To serve, cut from corner to corner, then cut from side to side, creating 8 wedges.

Rich Chocolate Cake,
Piedmont Style

RECOMMENDED WINE: **Moscato d'Asti**
ALTERNATIVE WINE: **Malvasia delle Lipari**

Here's more proof that simplest is best. Every mother and grand-mother in the Piedmont makes this marvelous dessert, called *bunet* (pronounced "bonnet"), and most restaurants serve it, too. Sometimes it's more of a pudding, sometimes more of a cake, but it's always richly delicious and easy to make. This version is from the Vajra family, whose brand-new winery in Barolo I first visited in the mid-1980s, in the same week that I finished almost every meal with this dessert and nearly became a chocoholic. The affinity of chocolate and spicy sweet wine is beautifully demonstrated by these two choices, one from the home ground, and the other from Lipari.

6 large eggs

6 tablespoons superfine sugar

2 cups milk

½ cup crumbled amaretti cookies

3 tablespoons unsweetened cocoa powder

2 tablespoons rum (optional)

¼ cup granulated sugar

2 tablespoons water

SERVES 6

PREHEAT THE OVEN TO 325°F.

IN A LARGE BOWL, beat together the eggs and superfine sugar until blended. Add the milk, cookies, cocoa, and rum (if using), and whisk to combine thoroughly. Set aside.

TO MAKE A CARAMELIZED COATING FOR THE TOP, put the granulated sugar and water in a small heavy-bottomed saucepan and place over medium-low heat. Heat, stirring with a wooden spoon, until the sugar melts, about 10 minutes. Continue to heat until the sugar turns golden brown and is completely smooth, another 2 to 3 minutes. Remove from the heat, pour into the bottom of a ring-shaped 1-quart dessert mold, and tilt the pan from side to side to spread the coating evenly. It will set quickly.

POUR THE EGG MIXTURE INTO THE MOLD. Place the mold in a roasting pan and pour hot water into the pan to reach halfway up the sides of the mold. Bake the cake until a toothpick or wooden skewer inserted into its center comes out clean, about 40 minutes. Remove to a rack and let cool completely.

TO UNMOLD, dip the base of the mold briefly in hot water, invert a plate on top, and invert the mold and plate together. Tap the base of the mold lightly with the back of a wooden spoon and lift it off. Cut the cake into wedges to serve.

Zuppa Inglese
with Strawberries

RECOMMENDED WINE: **Prosecco Extra Dry**

ALTERNATIVE WINE: **Asti Spumante**

For reasons no one is entirely sure of, the name of this gloriously sensual dessert translates as "English soup." It is similar to the famous English trifle, but a considerable improvement on that sherry-drenched, soggy concoction, and a lot more vibrant than its upstart cousin, the recently arrived but already clichéd tiramisu. The best *zuppa inglese* I've had was made with strawberries, which also makes it a perfect partner for the light and lively sparkler of the Veneto, Prosecco. Together, they're an easy, but modestly elegant, way to end a meal. If fresh strawberries aren't available, frozen are acceptable, but you must drain them after thawing, so they don't make the cake soggy. You can always drizzle a little of the juice in an attractive pattern on top of the final layer of cream.

4 large egg yolks

¼ cup granulated sugar

pinch of salt

1 cup milk

2 cups heavy cream

1 vanilla bean, split in half lengthwise

2 tablespoons Grand Marnier

1 sponge cake, 9 inches in diameter, 2 inches thick

½ cup sweet Marsala

1 pound strawberries, hulled and sliced,
   plus more for garnish

½ cup crushed amaretti cookies

2 tablespoons superfine sugar

toasted sliced almonds for garnish (optional)

SERVES 8

IN A BOWL, combine the egg yolks, granulated sugar, and salt. Beat with a whisk or handheld electric mixer until smooth and creamy. In a heavy-bottomed saucepan, combine the milk, 1 cup of the cream, and the vanilla bean and heat over medium-low heat until bubbles begin to appear around the edge of the pan. Remove from the heat and discard the vanilla bean. Slowly pour ½ cup of the hot milk mixture into the egg mixture while whisking. Then slowly whisk the egg mixture into the saucepan. Place the saucepan over low heat and cook, whisking constantly, until the custard thickens to a lightly creamy consistency. This may take as long as 20 minutes. Do not let it boil or even simmer. Remove from the heat and add the Grand Marnier. Pour into a bowl, cover, and refrigerate until chilled.

THIS IS BEST CONSTRUCTED IN A 9-INCH ROUND CLEAR GLASS DISH, which will show the layers, but a 9-inch soufflé dish will also do. Cut the sponge cake horizontally into 2 equal layers. They will each be about 1 inch thick. Place a layer in the bottom of the dish (if necessary, trim to fit). Sprinkle half the Marsala over the layer. Top with half the strawberries and then the amaretti crumbs. Spread half the custard over the top. Place the remaining cake layer on top, and then the remaining Marsala, strawberries, and custard. Cover and chill for 3 to 4 hours.

REMOVE FROM THE REFRIGERATOR 30 MINUTES BEFORE SERVING. It should be only lightly chilled when brought to the table. Just before serving, in a bowl, combine the remaining 1 cup cream and the superfine sugar and whip until soft peaks form. Spread the cream over the top custard layer. Garnish the top with sliced strawberries or almonds (if desired). To serve, scoop out carefully with a large serving spoon.

Double Chocolate Fantasia
with Coffee Zabaglione

RECOMMENDED WINE: **Moscato d'Asti**
ALTERNATIVE WINE: **Moscato di Pantelleria**

One of the many contradictions of Italy is that although Italians generally aren't big on dessert, they are crazy about chocolate, so it becomes the magnificent exception. Heinz Beck, the flamboyantly talented star chef of the Cavalieri Hilton Hotel in Rome, came up with this extravagant example of "give 'em what they want," a chocoholic's top note if ever there was one. I've adapted and slightly simplified it, though I took his advice and used Amadei chocolate after a sampling of its flavor left me weak in the knees.

CHOCOLATE SQUARES:

8 ounces bittersweet chocolate
 (at least 70 percent cacao), chopped

MOUSSE:

8 ounces white chocolate

3 large egg yolks

1 tablespoon superfine sugar

1 cup heavy cream

COFFEE ZABAGLIONE:

3 large egg yolks

3 tablespoons superfine sugar

3 tablespoons brewed espresso

SERVES 4

TO MAKE THE CHOCOLATE SQUARES, select a heatproof bowl that will rest in the top of a saucepan and put the chocolate into it. Pour water to a depth of about 2 inches into the saucepan and bring to a bare simmer. Place the bowl of chocolate over—not touching—the barely simmering water and allow the chocolate to melt slowly (this will take 10 or 12 minutes). Stir the chocolate until smooth, then remove the bowl from over the water and place it on a folded kitchen towel. Let cool.

LAY A LONG SHEET OF PARCHMENT PAPER ON A WORK SURFACE. Warm a spatula or long-bladed knife by pouring boiling water over it and then drying it thoroughly. Pour the chocolate onto the parchment. Working quickly, spread the chocolate using a troweling motion (it will have the consistency of thick emulsion paint) into a 6-by-8-inch rectangle, about $\frac{1}{8}$ inch thick. It should be as even as possible. Keeping the sheet flat, put it aside in a cool place (not the refrigerator) until the chocolate sets.

TO MAKE THE MOUSSE, melt the white chocolate in a heatproof bowl using the same technique as above. Remove from the heat and set aside. Put the egg yolks and sugar in another heatproof bowl and place over the barely simmering water in the saucepan. Whisk until foamy and firm enough to hold a peak (a handheld electric mixer will save time and energy here), about 12 minutes. Remove from the heat and let cool, about 10 minutes. Using a rubber spatula, gently fold the white chocolate into the yolk mixture, being careful not to deflate it. Let cool further and then chill lightly, 15 to 20 minutes.

IN A BOWL, whip the cream until it holds soft peaks. Scoop up one-third of the cream and gently fold it into the chilled chocolate mixture. Repeat with the remaining cream in 2 batches. Cover and chill until ready to assemble the layers.

CHILL 4 SMALL PLATES IN THE REFRIGERATOR FOR 30 MINUTES. Remove the mousse from the refrigerator. With a very sharp knife, cut the dark chocolate sheet into squares measuring about $1\frac{1}{4}$ inches. Using a small spatula or butter knife, lift a square from the paper and place it on a plate. Spoon a heaping teaspoon of white chocolate mousse on top of it, then add another square of dark chocolate, pressing down lightly. Continue until you have made a stack 6 squares tall. Repeat to make 3 more stacks on the remaining plates. (This can be done an hour or two ahead. Cover the plates lightly with plastic wrap and refrigerate. Refrigerate the remaining mousse as well.)

JUST BEFORE SERVING, make the coffee zabaglione. Put the egg yolks and sugar in a heatproof bowl and place over barely simmering water in a saucepan as before. Whisk until the mixture begins to foam. Whisking constantly, add the espresso little by little, continuing to whisk until a foamy mass the consistency of whipped cream forms. Remove from the heat. Spoon the zabaglione around the stacks in an attractive pattern. Place a dot of white chocolate mousse on top of each stack and serve at once.

Almond **Biscotti**

RECOMMENDED WINE: **Vin Santo**
ALTERNATIVE WINE: **Moscato di Pantelleria**

This is a simple version of the cookies known as biscotti (or *cantucci* in Tuscany) that are served after meals. They are presented alongside a glass of sweet wine, into which they're dunked to soften. Sometimes they are accompanied with a bit of cheese and walnuts or dried chestnuts as well. A good many variations of this recipe are possible. For example, you could mix in a little chopped crystallized ginger or some chocolate chips, or a sprinkle of ground cinnamon or fennel seeds. If you prefer the cookies softer, simply omit the second baking; the loaves can be sliced a few minutes after they're taken out of the oven and the cookies laid on a wire rack to cool.

1 cup whole almonds
1 ½ cups all-purpose flour
1 ¼ cups superfine sugar
½ teaspoon baking soda
pinch of salt
2 large eggs, beaten

MAKES ABOUT 24 COOKIES

PREHEAT THE OVEN TO 350°F.

SPREAD THE ALMONDS ON A BAKING SHEET AND TOAST IN THE OVEN UNTIL THEY ARE FRAGRANT AND LIGHTLY BROWNED, about 8 to 10 minutes. (Remember, they'll keep cooking for 1 or 2 minutes after being removed from the oven, so be careful not to let them get too brown.) Pour onto a plate to cool, then chop roughly. Leave the oven set at 350°F.

SIFT THE FLOUR INTO A LARGE BOWL. Add the sugar, baking soda, salt, and almonds and stir well. Add the eggs and mix with a wooden spoon until a soft, elastic dough forms. Turn the dough out onto a lightly floured work surface and divide into 6 pieces. Shape each portion into a small loaf about 4 inches long, 2 ½ inches wide, and 1 inch high. Place the loaves on a lightly oiled baking sheet.

BAKE THE LOAVES UNTIL THEY ARE A LIGHT GOLDEN BROWN, about 25 minutes. Remove from the oven, let cool slightly on the baking sheet, and then, with a spatula, transfer the loaves to a cutting board. Using a serrated knife, cut the loaves crosswise into ½-inch-thick slices. Place the slices, cut side down, on the baking sheet (you may have to do this in 2 batches).

RETURN TO THE OVEN AND BAKE UNTIL DEEP GOLDEN BROWN, about 10 minutes. Remove the slices to wire racks to cool. They will keep in an airtight container for up to 2 weeks.

Foundations

Building Blocks

Good restaurants always have plenty of staples
prepared in advance, things like stocks, sauces, and
flavoring components made in the quiet times of
the day. They are building blocks for many dishes
and are also great time-savers, making them invaluable
when you're entertaining. Here are a few of my building
blocks, which are used in several recipes in this book.

Pesto

1 cup tightly packed fresh basil leaves

1 large clove garlic, coarsely chopped

2 tablespoons pine nuts

½ cup extra-virgin olive oil

2 tablespoons grated Parmesan cheese

salt

MAKES 1 ¾ CUPS

IN A FOOD PROCESSOR, combine the basil, garlic, and pine nuts. Pulse to chop and mix the ingredients. Add ¼ cup of the olive oil and process for 1 minute. Then add the remaining ¼ cup olive oil and the cheese and process to make a smooth sauce. Taste for salt (a pinch or two may bring out the flavor of the cheese).

THE SAUCE SHOULD BE MORE OF A LIQUID THAN A PURÉE; if you need to add more olive oil, put the sauce into a bowl and whisk the oil in by hand, a tablespoon at a time. Store, tightly covered, in the refrigerator for up to a week.

Chickpea Sauce,
Lucchese Style

Buca di Sant'Antonio is the oldest and arguably the best restaurant in the Tuscan walled city of Lucca, serving traditional regional food since 1782 in an attractive and slightly whimsical setting. (The ceiling is hung with old copper cooking implements and brass musical instruments, including a couple of tubas.) A specialty of the region and the restaurant is an antipasto of vegetable pies and tarts, served with this rich sauce, which has a deep, nutty flavor. I have included a recipe for one of the pies on page 99, but this sauce is so versatile that it has many other uses.

> 1 ½ cups (8 ounces) dried chickpeas
>
> 2 cups homemade chicken stock or
> reduced-sodium canned chicken broth
>
> 1 bay leaf
>
> 3 tablespoons extra-virgin olive oil
>
> salt and freshly ground black pepper

MAKES ABOUT 3 ½ CUPS

SOAK THE CHICKPEAS IN COLD WATER TO COVER OVERNIGHT. Drain, rinse, and place in a heavy-bottomed saucepan. Add the stock and bay leaf and bring to a slow, but steady simmer over medium heat. Cover and cook until tender, about 1 hour.

REMOVE FROM THE HEAT AND DISCARD THE BAY LEAF. Let cool slightly, then put the chickpeas and their cooking liquid in a blender (you may have to do it in batches). Add the olive oil and process until the mixture is a smooth purée. Season with salt and pepper. Cover and refrigerate until ready to use.

VARIATIONS:

Whisk 3 tablespoons grated pecorino cheese into 1 cup of the sauce as you reheat it, and pour over broccoli or cauliflower, for example, and turn those dullards into something special. Or add 1 tablespoon chopped fresh sage and several generous grinds of black pepper to the sauce and drizzle it over grilled mixed vegetables. You can also stir 1 cup chopped tomatoes into 1 cup of the sauce, heat, and toss with chopped steamed spinach for a robust side dish. The other virtue of this sauce is that it will keep for up to 2 weeks in a jar in the fridge, so it's easily ready to be used or transformed.

Tomato Essence

Commercial sun-dried tomatoes packed in olive oil often vary in quality, so I prefer to make my own concentrated essence of tomato, which I find delivers a lot more flavor.

2 pounds cherry tomatoes

salt

6 tablespoons olive oil

2 tablespoons finely chopped garlic

6 tablespoons finely chopped fresh parsley

1/2 teaspoon sugar

1 cup water, or as needed

MAKES ABOUT 1 CUP

YOU WILL NEED 2 SKILLETS OR A LARGE HEAVY-BOTTOMED ROASTING PAN. Cut the tomatoes in half crosswise. Sprinkle the cut sides with salt. Brush the bottom of each skillet with 2 tablespoons of the olive oil or use 4 tablespoons for the roasting pan. Put the tomatoes in the pan(s), cut side down, and place over medium-low heat until they release their juices. Off the heat, turn the tomatoes over and evenly scatter the garlic, parsley, and sugar over them. Turn the heat down to its lowest setting, return the pan(s) to the heat, and slowly cook the tomatoes. Add 1/4 cup warm water each time they dry out. After 20 to 30 minutes and 3 to 4 additions of warm water, the tomatoes will begin to caramelize. Scrape the bottom of the pan(s) with a wooden spoon to loosen the browned bits.

WHEN THE TOMATOES ARE THOROUGHLY COOKED DOWN AND ONLY A LITTLE LIQUID REMAINS, remove them from the heat and place in a bowl. Stir in the remaining 2 tablespoons olive oil, allow to cool, and place in an airtight jar. The essence will keep for up to a week in the refrigerator.

Salt Cod

Salt cod is quite wonderful, and despite its name is not very salty. It has a satisfying firmness, and I often make hash with it, simply frying flakes of the cod with cooked potatoes and parsley, or I add it to simple tomato sauce for a more interesting supper. Store-bought salt cod is often expensive and the quality can be variable. It's easy, and better, to make your own.

FILL A SHALLOW OVAL OR RECTANGULAR DISH (I use a glass baking dish) with kosher salt to a depth of $\frac{1}{2}$ inch. Place a skinless cod fillet on top of it, and pour more kosher salt over the top, burying the fish in a layer of salt $\frac{1}{2}$ inch deep. Cover the dish with plastic wrap and leave for 1 week in the refrigerator. The salt will form a crust and then a kind of slurry, as it draws the water out of the fish. The fish will shrink a little and firm up.

TO USE THE SALT COD, remove it from the dish and discard the salt. Rinse the fish and the dish, and return the fish to the dish with cold water to cover. Place in the refrigerator for 2 days, changing the water twice daily. The salt cod is then ready to use. This method also works well for any flaky fish—haddock is quite good, for example, and it restores texture to many fish that are usually sold previously frozen, like orange roughy.

Olive Marmalade

Thousands of years ago, the Etruscans (often thought of as the original Italians) were wiped out by the upstart Romans, so thoroughly that very little is known about them. The mystery keeps people coming to Etruria, the hilly land north of Rome in the province of Lazio, to explore the archeological sites and museums. One of the most notable visitors was D. H. Lawrence, who wrote a book about the area in 1930, and took his meals at a café there run by the grandmother of Fulvio Ferri. Fulvio is well known as a businessman and politician, but I know him as a fine cook, generous with family recipes. This one works well as a relish, alongside grilled fish for example; as a topping for bruschetta (with Orvieto or Est! Est!! Est!!!, for example); or as a flavoring ingredient, as in Osteria alle Testiere's fish simmered in wine (page 64).

1 pound olive oil–packed
    green olives, pitted and
    roughly chopped
6 cloves garlic, minced
grated zest of 1 lemon
juice of 1 lemon
grated zest of 2 oranges
1 tablespoon chopped fresh sage
½ tablespoon chopped fresh rosemary
½ teaspoon salt
½ cup olive oil

MAKES ABOUT 4 CUPS

IN A LARGE BOWL, combine all the ingredients except the olive oil and mix thoroughly. In a large heavy-bottomed saucepan, heat ¼ cup of the olive oil over medium heat. Add the olive mixture to the pan, reduce the heat to medium-low, and simmer, uncovered, stirring occasionally, for 1 hour. Remove from the heat and let cool.

POUR THE OLIVE MIXTURE INTO A FOOD PROCESSOR AND PULSE A FEW TIMES TO PURÉE LIGHTLY. Place in a jar, pour the remaining ¼ cup olive oil in a layer over the top, cover, and store in the refrigerator. It will keep well for a couple of weeks.

Olive **Oil**

Five of us were gathered around a small table at a little restaurant downstairs from the Communist Party headquarters in Alba, the heart of the Piedmont's wine country. Four of us were wine and food writers, the fifth a local winemaker, and everybody was excited except me. Why? Because we were about to participate in an olive oil tasting. I go to wine tastings all the time, and I do taste comparisons with wine at home all the time, so this should have been easy, but I was nervous. My fellow judges had been showing off all day in preparation for this tasting, one-upping each other about Ligurian smoothness versus Tuscan pepperiness, and I didn't know my Ascolano from my Pendulino — back home in California, I cooked with peanut oil and made salad dressing with sunflower oil (or whatever else was considered healthiest at the moment).

Eventually, six olive oils were brought out in the sort of shallow little ceramic dishes that have now become commonplace in trendy restaurants in the United States, along with a basket of little pieces of bread. We had our blind tasting, dipping the bread in the oils and making notes, and murmuring and ponderously hmmmmming, and there was more one-upmanship, and then finally we had a very nice dinner.

I had been surprised and pleased to discover that I really liked some of the flavors and felt I wanted to learn more (but by myself), and I got through the discussion fairly easily by basically agreeing with everything said by the most outspoken of my colleagues. That was twenty years ago, and it turned out to be the first step in a pleasant, easygoing journey I'm still happy to be on.

Choosing

Olive trees are long-lived evergreens that can grow in a band of temperate zones around the world (just like grapes), and there are more varieties of olives than can be counted. A few of the more expensive "gourmet" olive oils now declare what varieties they're made from on the back label, but most of the time, we're offered an anonymous blend—it's a little like having to choose only from "dry white" or "dry red" wine. The solution is much the same as with wine, in fact: get as much information as possible from the label, find a reputable retailer and ask for advice, and finally, taste and taste again.

One problem with olive oil is the standard of labeling, which often has vague or unhelpful nomenclature. There are five grades. *Extra-virgin* is the finest, fruitiest, and lowest in acidity, less than 1 percent; it can be green and unfiltered, or clear and greenish golden. *Virgin* and *fino* are slightly higher in acidity, and not commonly seen outside Italy. *Olive oil* is made from refined oil that has been de-acidified and then blended with a little extra-virgin or virgin oil. *Light olive oil* is filtered, lighter in color, fragrance, and flavor (but not calories). Its only advantage is that it burns or smokes at a higher temperature than the other olive oils. On the other hand, if you want a neutral oil that doesn't burn easily (if you're browning meat that will be further cooked, as in stew, or large batches of vegetables), sunflower oil is cheaper and more effective. It's what the Italians typically use to save money.

Beyond those terms, any other information is voluntary. There will be a sell-by date, but that's usually two years after bottling, which is too generous.

Right now, I have seven olive oils in my larder, all Italian, including one truffle oil, which, being flavored, is a different sort of thing altogether. One simple "olive oil," a moderately priced popular brand I get at the supermarket, declares itself "100% pure olive oil" and "Italian," which is, I suppose, a reasonable minimum. I use it for cooking, and it tastes all right.

I chose it by buying several small bottles of different inexpensive brands and using them before choosing the best one. Then I bought it in a larger economy size to use as my everyday oil. The other five are "extra virgin." Two, from Apulia, declare that they're unfiltered and show a harvest date, which is useful—olive oil is only good for at most a year. The one from Umbria tells me the harvest date, the region it's from, and that it's DOC (a denomination of origin, with some standards set), which is at least a bit reassuring. The one from Tuscany tells me the farm-estate where it was bottled and when, and that it's DOC. The label on the Sicilian tells me the whole story: the three varieties of olives used, when and where they were harvested, their acidity, how they taste, and how to use the oil.

Which is best? Well, neither the most nor the least informative. One of the oils from Apulia and the Sicilian are full flavored; that is, they taste distinctly like olive oil, but they're simple. I use them to make salad dressing or drizzle alone on strong-flavored salad (one with arugula or endive or a lot of onions in it). The oil from Umbria is slightly spicy and is my utility extra-virgin, middle-of-the-road choice, useful everywhere. The other Apulian and the Tuscan are distinctly spicy; I use them as a condiment, to add zip to soup, straight on salad (I seldom make vinaigrette or other type of intrusive salad dressing anymore, as the flavor of good oil seems better), or brushed onto toast for bruschetta. All the extra-virgin oils are fairly expensive, and the latter three are worth it, although nothing on the labels told me they would be as good as they are—one was a gift from an Italian friend, and the other two were recommended by the guy at the Italian deli down the street, his judgment confirmed when I tasted them. *It's the only way.*

When it comes to wine, olive oil provides another benefit: compatibility, either when used in cooking, as a condiment, or for dressing a salad. Its lightness, smoothness, and subtle flavors make olive oil very wine friendly.

The Basics

Olive oil should be stored in a cupboard, in the dark most of the time, in a relatively cool place, and is at its best for six months. It will be quite good for longer if stored in the fridge, and may become cloudy (a harmless development; it may also become cloudy in cool weather) and too thick to pour easily. Unfiltered olive oil will often deposit a light green sediment, which is also harmless. It's certainly among the most digestible of oils. It's monounsaturated and has no cholesterol, and is considered to be quite healthful, although it's somewhat high in calories (125 calories to a tablespoonful, though obviously in cooking you're not going to ingest all that you use).

Experts taste olive oil by pouring a little into thin glasses, warming the glasses with their hands, and then smelling and sipping it. Dipping bread into it is easier and not a bad way to do it, as long as the bread is very bland. The best way to taste oils was given to me by a cook: Pour a few drops into the palm of your hand, rub it with your finger to warm it, take a good sniff, and then lick it off your hand and roll it around in your mouth. If you're trying a few oils, refresh your palate with a bite of apple or a sip of white wine in between tastes and dry your hand with a paper towel. It's quite an effective method.

NOTE: *In this book, I occasionally specify extra-virgin olive oil in cooking. The reason is that the chefs who gave me the recipes were adamant about using it, and the cooking times are so short that it might make sense to use the more expensive version since the flavor will not be totally lost. On the other hand, chefs can get a bit mystical about their art. I don't see a big difference, and I think you should use what you think is best, and can afford.*

Italian **Cheese**

Italy was unified into a nation late in the nineteenth century, but it wasn't until nearly a hundred years later that Italians started to travel widely around their own country and discover the finer points of one another's regional cuisines, especially when it came to localized and highly specific products such as wine and cheese. Given that history of fragmentation, it's no surprise that few Italian cheeses ever built any sort of international reputation, except by hearsay. (It's also ridiculously ironic, given that the Romans passed along many of their cheesemaking secrets to the French and Swiss more than two thousand years ago.) The few cheeses that did become famous, such as *Parmigiano-Reggiano,* provolone, pecorino, and mozzarella, were sometimes victims of their success, with inferior industrialized versions dumped on export markets, or imitations poorly copied by U.S. mass-marketers, which dragged down their reputations. At last, that's been changing. Italy has more than four hundred cheeses to offer, many as good as anything from anywhere else, and they're not staying home anymore. For cooking and for eating, we have a delicious array of superb choices, enhanced by wine. Here's a primer on the most popular versions, with some wine recommendations.

Asiago

Made for nearly a thousand years, Asiago is a cow's milk cheese from the Veneto with a slightly sweet, nutty flavor. There are basically two versions, made in two different ways: *Asiago pressato* is white, made from full-cream milk, so it has a fairly high fat content and supple, smooth texture. It's a delicious table cheese, in other words meant to be eaten. *Asiago d'allevo* is made from a blend of two milkings of the cows (morning and evening, with the first batch, which is also skimmed, allowed to stand for at least six hours and acquire some piquancy). The cheese is matured slowly, gaining flavor and a bit of sharpness. When young (a few months old), it's very pale yellow, and good eating; as it ages, up to two years, it darkens, hardens, becomes grainy, and develops intense flavor. Up to a year old, while it's still al dente, it's still good eating, and a fine partner for medium red wines such as Valpolicella Classico. After that, as it becomes very hard, it's brilliant for cooking and for grating over pasta or polenta.

Caciocavallo

Originally made exclusively in southern Italy and with a history that goes back to the Middle Ages, *caciocavallo* is easily recognizable by its distinctive pear shape, with several small cheeses often tied together with string around their necks. (The cheeses are hung over poles to mature, and the name—"horse cheese"—probably comes from their resemblance to saddlebags.) It's a cow's milk cheese, made by allowing the curd to ripen for a few days, until it reaches a perceptible level of acidity. It is then washed and stretched in warm water, after which it is cut into chunks and kneaded and shaped in cold water until it's firm. The aroma is intense and the flavor is lingering, but fairly mellow, with a moderate tangy bite.

Caciocavallo is made in all the southern regions (Calabria, Campania, Molise, Basilicata, and Apulia), and on several of the southern islands, and is mostly eaten as table cheese. It is good with the new generation of southern reds like Negroamaro or Nero d'Avola. The Sicilian versions are unique, shaped into either squares or rectangles, and a bit more tangy. They are used more for cooking, sometimes grated into rich dishes in broth, and sometimes on their own, rolled in bread crumbs and fried.

Castelmagno

Castelmagno is something of a heritage cheese from the Piedmont region, highly regarded since the thirteenth century (when it was even used as currency), somewhat neglected in much of the twentieth, and now revived and deservedly popular again. It's a blue cheese, but fairly low in fat, not very saturated with the characteristic blue veins of mold, and relatively mild. It's made from cow's milk, with some goat's and sheep's milk added, and is a blend of two milkings, so although its flavor is milder than many blue cheeses, it has some complexity and character. Most of the time it's sold fairly young, before any mold develops, as a tasty and tangy table cheese. But it's worth seeking out an aged version: it may look like a rough, hard lump, but inside it's persistently flavored, pungent, and noble. The young version is a good match with a lightly sweet white such as a Vin Santo, while the older type would be best with Amarone.

Dolcelatte

Dolcelatte is as nice as it sounds (the name means "sweet milk"). It's a commercial cheese, produced in industrial quantities, ignored by cheese snobs, but it's amiable, easygoing, and deliciously creamy. It's soft and smooth, almost melting in your mouth, impossible to resist. Basically, *dolcelatte* is a baby blue cheese, a sort of younger sibling to Gorgonzola, but made from only one milking of the cows and only lightly matured before being sold. It's rich and mild at the same time, and has a fat content of around 50 percent. Aside from being a pleasant cheese to snack on, it's often stirred into hot pasta for a quick and certainly filling informal meal. It's also sometimes known as *Gorgonzola dolce*.

Dolcelatte torta, which was first concocted in the 1960s, is not really a tart, but rather layers of *dolcelatte* alternating with mascarpone cream. It's almost too much, rich and creamy and absolutely sinful, quite delicious, but at 75 percent fat content, a little goes a long way. It's terrific spread on toast or tossed with hot pasta, though too rich to be wine friendly.

Fontina

Fontina is one of Italy's best cheeses, made from the milk of pampered cows that graze on the lush green grass of the high mountain pastures of Valle d'Aosta on the edge of the Alps, north of the Piedmont. It's made from fresh, unpasteurized milk from a single milking, and all the steps of the cheesemaking process are carried out quickly, to preserve its distinct, slightly sweet and nutty flavor. It is then aged in cool, damp, natural surroundings—caves, tunnels, former army bunkers, even an old copper mine—for at least three months. Fontina's firmness belies its richness—it's semisoft and only slightly elastic, and has a fat content of about 45 percent—but that richness and superb flavor make it versatile, especially in cooking. When melted, it becomes the basis for *fonduta,* the superior Italian version of fondue, and it's often cooked together with veal or pasta. As a table cheese, it's the cornerstone of any cheese board, and a good partner for crisp white wines like Gavi or Vernaccia di San Gimignano.

Gorgonzola

One of the great blue cheeses of the world, with a history going back centuries, Gorgonzola is made in the northern regions of Lombardy and Piedmont. Cow's milk is pasteurized and inoculated with the *Penicillium roqueforti* mold and, after settling, goes to "purgatory," which in this case is a very damp, very warm room where the mold takes hold and the cheese ripens quickly. Later, the cheeses are pierced with needles, a step that encourages the spread of the mold and the development of the characteristic complex flavors that make blue cheeses so fascinating—it's creamy and piquant at the same time, rich but has some bite of acidity, and is up-front yet lingering. The usual wine choice is Amarone, which is equally complex, direct, and big in flavor (the combination is something of a gastronomic Clash of the Titans); a more subtle match is with Recioto di Soave, whose light sweetness and tingle of acidity provide a cushion for the richness of the cheese. The sweet version (called *passito*) of Sagrantino di Montefalco is also worth a try.

Mascarpone

Technically, mascarpone isn't a cheese, but instead more like heavy cultured cream (or yogurt without the bite). It's more or less in the family, sold in the cheese section of stores, and used like cheese sometimes as an ingredient in ravioli filling or in sauces. Originally from Lombardy in the north, it's now become so popular (thanks partly to the fashion for tiramisu) that it's produced in several areas; there's even a version from the south made from buffalo's milk. Rich and high in fat (more than 50 percent, often up to 75 percent), it works well in both sweet and savory foods, but isn't terribly wine friendly.

Montasio

Montasio is becoming increasingly popular, with good reason—it's got good, sturdy, fairly complex flavor, with a tang of acidity reminiscent of a fruit, like pineapple. Though it's a firm cow's milk cheese, its richness makes it seem creamy. It's from the northeastern corner of Italy, Friuli and the Veneto, and when aged between three and twelve months as a table cheese, it makes a good partner to the moderately light red wines of both regions, such as Refosco, Valpolicella, or Schioppettino, and even the lightly herbal Sauvignon Blanc from Friuli. When aged for more than a year, it becomes hard, more tangy, slightly grainy, and makes a good, crunchy snack. *Montasio* is widely used for cooking, grated over pasta, polenta, and carpaccio; in sauces; or fried into the delicious snack called *frico* (page 97).

Mozzarella

Real mozzarella, made from buffalo's milk and known as *mozzarella di bufala,* deserves better than to be sliced and slapped onto a pizza. In southern Italy, it's serious table cheese, often served as part of the antipasto, with a little extra-virgin olive oil drizzled over it, or perhaps a few drops of balsamic vinegar. It's usually bought on the day it's made and is eaten as fresh as possible. Good mozzarella has a subtle but distinct flavor, slightly nutty and milky, and a moist, springy texture (the rubbery stuff that goes on pizza is usually cow's milk mozzarella made on an industrial scale in large blocks). There aren't enough buffalo to satisfy the demand, and the next best thing is organic cow's milk versions, which can be quite good. There are also smoked versions, called *affumicata* or *scamorza,* toasty golden brown on the outside, and tasty but a bit chewy. Alas, no version is much of a match with wine.

Parmigiano-Reggiano, Grana Padano, and *Grana*

If I were limited to only one kind of cheese for the rest of my life, it would have to be *Parmigiano-Reggiano,* the delicious apex of cheese making, the top of the hard-cheese heap. Carefully made, its reputation zealously protected, it is generally acknowledged, even by the French, as one of the great cheeses of the world. At formal, grand occasions in Italy, you often see a whole sixty-five-pound wheel of *Parmigiano-Reggiano,* its top broken into with a special wedge-shaped knife that breaks off pieces like lumps of granite, meant to be nibbled with Champagne (a superb match, by the way). It's lavish, and appropriate, befitting the status of the cheese and certainly making the guests feel pretty elevated, too.

What's amazing, considering the richness of its flavor, is that the cheese is made partly from skimmed milk, which is mixed with whole milk from a second milking (the cream taken off the first milking is made into mascarpone). Everything about this cheese is regulated, and for the best: it can only come from specific parts of Emilia-Romagna, the cows may only be fed grass or hay, aging takes at least twelve months, and no additives are allowed. The cheesemaking process is painstaking, involving more than two dozen steps before aging even begins, but the result is unique, hard and granular, sweet and slightly fruity, rich and full but never biting, good to eat, great to grate, wonderful to cook with. As if that weren't enough, it even freezes well (and can be grated frozen, too).

Grana padano is a similar cheese in every way except that it comes from a broader area (parts of Lombardy, the Piedmont, the Veneto, Trentino, and Emilia-Romagna) and is less stringently regulated. It's still a fine cheese, just a notch down from the *Parmigiano* peak. It also costs less, though it's not cheap. The relatively inexpensive generic version is simply called *grana,* made along the length of the Po River valley in northern Italy. It's pretty darn good, too.

Much of the time, these cheeses are all referred to as "Parmesan," which has its limits as a catch-all name, mostly in that it has no legally enforceable definition. The three cheeses just named are all too good and way too expensive to be sold grated in little boxes or canisters; I don't know what's really in them, and don't use them. You should, as a rule, only buy Parmesan-type cheeses in whole chunks, where you know what you're buying, spending as much as you can afford, and grate it yourself. Life's too short to eat inferior cheese.

NOTE: *In the recipes in this book, I've used Parmesan as an umbrella term for these cheeses, and occasionally Parmigiano-Reggiano if the chef who gave me the recipe insisted it made a difference and was adamant about using it. There's no doubt that the latter is superior, even when it's cooked, but there might be a question about how much, compared with its expense. I leave it to your discretion—and budget—to decide which suits you.*

Pecorino

Pecorino is actually a generic name for sheep's milk cheese, which is produced in several regions, each having slightly different characteristics; if you see a cheese labeled simply "pecorino," it's worth asking where it came from. *Pecorino romano* was a staple food of the Roman legionnaires, and probably one of the first cheeses to be exported from Italy. It's firm and white, slightly salty, with a noticeable tang. This is the version that's popular as grating cheese, as a little of it delivers a good kick of flavor. *Pecorino sardo* comes from Sardinia, where the seven million sheep considerably outnumber the people, and is an excellent table cheese when young, with a tangy flavor at once salty and slightly sweet; when aged, it becomes quite hard and is superb grated onto pasta. *Pecorino toscano* has an intense flavor that really blossoms when it's shaved onto pasta, risotto, or salads. A rare pecorino worth grabbing if you see it is *pecorino di fossa,* made in the hills of the Marches region, and aged in deep holes in the ground for three months, acquiring a woodsy aroma and flavor similar to mushrooms, earthy and delicious. Wines with crisp acidity and good fruit are the best match, especially whites like Gavi, really good Pinot Grigio, Sauvignon Blanc, or reds like Refosco or Schioppettino.

Provolone

Presliced and plastic-wrapped supermarket versions only give the slightest hint of what a good cheese this can be, deserving of a better fate than being crammed into a sandwich. Good-quality provolone, usually sausage shaped and tied up with string, is a versatile cheese, but probably best known as an ingredient in cooking, where its strongly tangy, even slightly funky, flavor boosts vegetable, chicken, and veal dishes. It's also very good eating when it's young, known as *provolone dolce.* The best way to judge its youth is to press on it. If it's springy and supple, it should be a treat, very pleasant with light red wines. As it ages, it becomes very firm, stronger, with a bit of spicy bite (the name for the aged version says it all—*piccante,* "piquant"). There is also a smoked version, a respectable cheese in its own right, which makes a nice snack. High-acid white wine with firm fruit, such as Pinot Bianco, Soave Classico, or good Pinot Grigio, is the best match.

Ricotta

If you've only tried ricotta in the flavorless cream cheese version sold in plastic tubs, you've missed out on just how fascinating and versatile it can be. Ricotta used to be made from leftovers (when cheese separates into solids, known as curds, and liquid, known as whey, some protein remains in the liquid and can be reclaimed by heating, which becomes *ricotta,* or "cooked again"). These days, in its mass-market versions, it's made from skimmed milk and is extremely bland. Used in cooking, it modifies and dilutes flavor, so it's useful mainly to thicken strong sauces.

The rest of the family is much more interesting, and worth seeking out. *Ricotta romana* or *ricotta gentile* is a by-product of pecorino cheese making, and gains a little character from the sheep's milk used, with a smooth and subtle flavor, best for cooking. For eating, *fior di ricotta,* made from sheep's milk, is fairly rich and almost buttery, wonderful spread on toast. Then there is a whole category of flavored versions: *Ricotta infornata,* from Sicily, looks like handmade dark bread; it's sprinkled with black pepper and then baked. *Ricotta mustia,* from Sardinia, is smoked with a mix of herbs, while *ricotta al fumo di ginepro,* from the Abruzzo, is smoked with juniper. Several types are called simply *ricotta affumicata,* with the area of origin attached. From Calabria, it's strong and heavily smoked with a mix of woods, while from the Veneto, pine wood is used for the smoking, with the addition of citric acid or vinegar to firm it up, which gives it a rather sharp bite. All these types are compatible with a wide range of medium-weight, fruity white wines. There are also versions that are salted and aged, mainly used grated on pasta and hearty soups.

Robiola

Robiola originated in Lombardy, where it was once made from goat's milk, though now it's also made in the Veneto and Piedmont regions, sometimes from cow's milk, but more often from a blend of goat's and cow's milk. It's soft and supple, mostly a table cheese eaten fairly young, with the characteristic sweet-sour-salty taste and tang of classic goat's milk cheese. It's rapidly gaining popularity, and the best versions are labeled with their origin, such as *robiola di Mondovi* or *robiola di Roccaverano,* sold in small flat cakes wrapped in waxy paper, as they can be very moist. A wine-friendly cheese, it's a nice match for very dry whites, such as Sauvignon Blanc, Gavi, Verdicchio, and Tocai Friulano, and even partners Vin Santo for an after-dinner treat.

Taleggio

Taleggio is easily recognized by its rosy crust and flat, square shape. It's one of Italy's few washed-rind cheeses, sponged down with brine to prevent the development of mold and a hard rind. The entire cheese is edible—the soft crust may not look appetizing, but it's fine. Most of it is made in large dairies across the north of Italy, but quality is strictly controlled. The top versions from the mountains near Lake Como are still matured deep in caves. When young, the cheese is rosy pink on the outside, slightly springy to the touch, with a gentle aroma reminiscent of sweet hay and nuts, and a buttery taste. As it ages, the color of the crust deepens to orange, the center becomes creamy, and the flavor is fuller, with a gentle but persistent tang. *Taleggio* matches well with a range of white wines, as long as they're aromatic and fruity: Pinot Bianco, Pinot Grigio, Lugana, and Arneis are especially good.

Toma

Toma is actually a large family of similar cheeses
mainly from the mountains of the Piedmont, with a
little from Valle d'Aosta and Liguria, which lie to the
north and south. When young (less than a year old,
and the type usually on the market), it's fresh and
creamy, with an echo of sweet green grass in the flavor
and a bit of tang. Most versions carry some sort of
geographic designation (*del Maccagno, di Lanzo,* or
Piemontese, for example). Although its flavor isn't
complex or striking, I've found that its variations are
all at least tasty, often quite straightforwardly good. It's
reliable, and goes well with fruity whites like Pinot
Grigio and Gavi.

Index

Table of **Equivalents**

The exact equivalents in the following tables have been rounded for convenience.

Liquid/Dry Measures

U.S.	¹⁄₄ **teaspoon**	¹⁄₂ **teaspoon**	1 teaspoon	1 tablespoon *(3 tsp)*	2 tablespoons *(1 fl oz)*
METRIC	1.25 milliliters	2.5 milliliters	5 milliliters	15 milliliters	30 milliliters
U.S.	¹⁄₄ **cup**	¹⁄₃ **cup**	¹⁄₂ **cup**	1 cup	
METRIC	60 milliliters	80 milliliters	120 milliliters	240 milliliters	
U.S.	1 pint *(2 cups)*	1 quart *(4 cups, 32 oz)*	1 gallon *(4 qts)*		
METRIC	480 milliliters	960 milliliters	3.84 liters		
U.S.	1 ounce *(by weight)*	1 pound	2.2 pounds		
METRIC	28 grams	454 grams	1 kilogram		

Length

U.S.	¹⁄₈ **inch**	¹⁄₄ **inch**	¹⁄₂ **inch**	1 inch
METRIC	3 millimeters	6 millimeters	12 millimeters	2.5 centimeters

Oven Temperature

FAHRENHEIT	250	275	300	325	350	375	400	425	450	475	500
CELSIUS	120	140	150	160	180	190	200	220	230	240	260
GAS	¹⁄₂	1	2	3	4	5	6	7	8	9	10